Text and diagrams

By Nick Robinson
with contributions by som
today's top origami designers

Photographs

Nick Robinson

Contents

Basic Dog
Traditional

page 20

Minimal Dog
Nick Robinson

page 26

Yoshizawa's Dog
Akira Yoshizawa

page 30

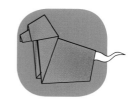

Alison's Dog
Nick Robinson

page 34

Scotty Dog
Robert Neale

page 40

Dogs
in Origami

NICK ROBINSON

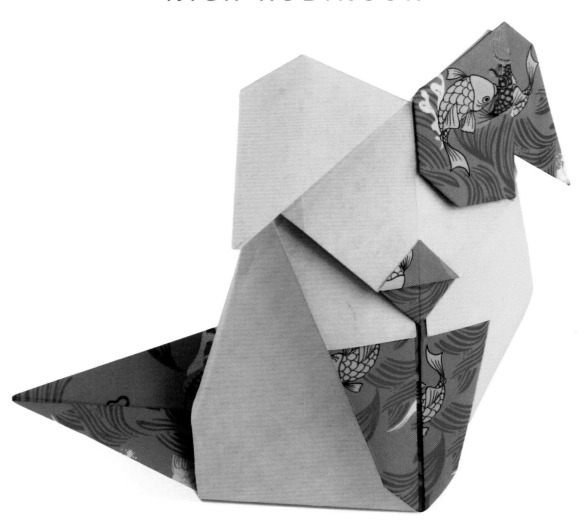

DOVER PUBLICATIONS, INC.
Mineola, New York

Bibliographical Note

Dogs in Origami, first published by Dover Publications, Inc., in 2019, is an unabridged English translation of the work originally published by NuiNui, Switzerland, in 2018.

International Standard Book Number

ISBN-13: 978-0-486-83230-2
ISBN-10: 0-486-83230-9

Manufactured in the United States by LSC Communications
83230901   2019
www.doverpublications.com

This book is dedicated to
Emeline Gilhooley and Martin Sommers

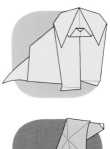
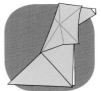

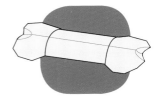

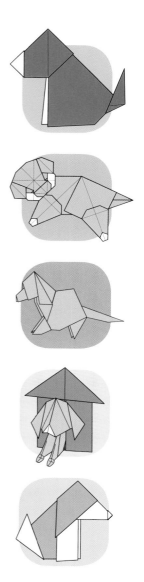

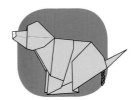

Introduction

Dogs are, of course "man's best friend," known for their loyalty. The domestic dog (*Canis familiaris*) is the most numerous carnivore on Earth. Dogs have lived with humans for as long as we can remember and they have formed a strong relationship with us. Dogs come in a range of widely different shapes, sizes and colors and perform many tasks for us, such as hunting, herding, pulling loads, protecting us, keeping us company and helping people with disabilities. Their marvelous sense of smell, sight, and hearing allow them to outperform humans in many areas.

Spending just half an hour with your dog can help you feel calmer and more relaxed, reducing stress and increasing happiness. Playing with your dog increases your brain's levels of dopamine and serotonin, both of which give a feeling of pleasure and tranquillity. Having a dog also improves your physical wellbeing and encourages a healthy lifestyle—your dog requires daily exercise, and so do you!

Dogs are intelligent creatures with a loyalty to their "human" that can be unexpectedly strong. They also bond with you and can sense your body language and emotions and feelings, and this helps to build an unbreakable relationship. Like their arch-enemy, cats, dogs are individuals, each with its own personality and character. No two dogs are the same, and as you live with them, you quickly learn to detect their moods and opinions. Yes, they have a few "bad habits," but so do their human owners, and you learn to love their imperfections because they are such good company.

In the world of origami, there are many, many dogs, representing a wide range of species. While you can model a specific type of dog (in this book we have a Bulldog, a Scotty Dog and an Alsatian), it's also possible to make a generic "dog" that everyone recognizes as such. As with most origami designs, these models allow you to make a large number of variations by adjusting angles and distances. There is an amazing range of paper patterns to try, although you shouldn't overlook plain paper—please experiment; there are no "rules" and paper is cheap.

How to fold

Folding paper neatly and accurately isn't always easy for newcomers to origami. However, there's no good reason why you can't progress in the subject, no matter how little confidence you have. A one-to-five paw rating appears on the first page of each project, indicating the difficulty level. Here are a few simple tips.

- Fold slowly—it's not a race. You will get much better results.
- It's generally better to fold the paper away from you rather than toward you (where you hands can get in the way).
- Set aside plenty of time to fold; it's not good for your concentration if you have distractions.
- Fold at a well-lit table, with enough space for your elbows and to follow the instructions in the book.
- Make all creases sharp to begin with, making sure the paper is perfectly positioned before flattening.
- Make each model at least 3 times using cheaper paper before using your best paper.
- If you make your own squares from a larger sheet, cut the paper as accurately as possible. A rotary trimmer is a good investment.
- Folding in a small group is fun and will also teach you a lot in a short time.
- Teaching the model to other people will really help your understanding of the folding sequence.

Choosing paper

Origami usually requires paper that is perfectly square. There are lots of options for "proper" origami paper (which can be bought cheaply on the internet), but you can also choose from many other types of paper, especially if you want to fold a large version of a model. The paper should be crisp and capable of "remembering" a crease (so it doesn't try to unfold itself). Craft and art shops have a huge range of beautiful papers—try to choose a pattern that really suits the final design. It will be better value to buy a large sheet then cut it down to make several smaller squares. Here is a simple method for creating a square from a rectangle.

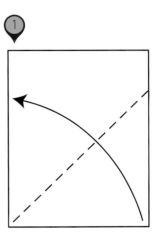

Fold a short edge to
a long edge.

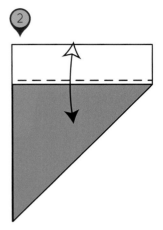

Fold the surplus
paper over the
edge, crease and
unfold.

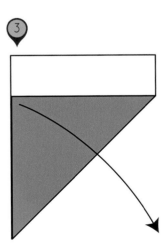

Unfold the paper fully.

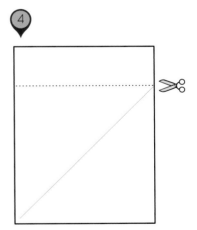

Cut off the surplus paper
to leave a square.

Techniques

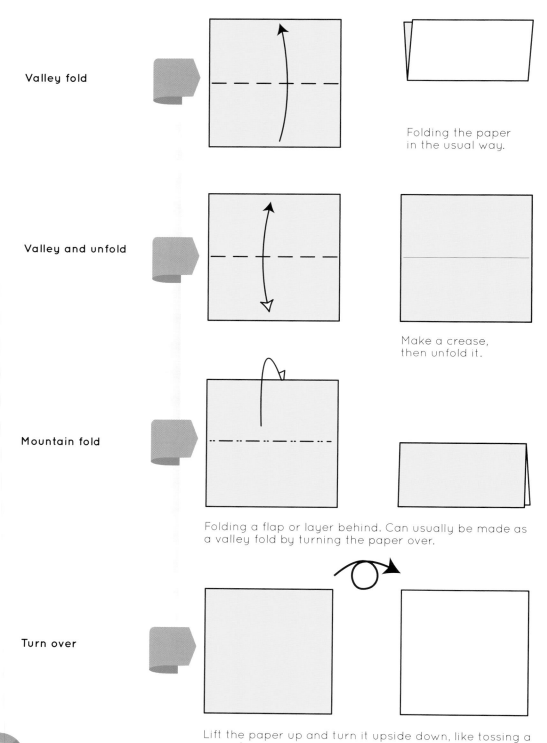

Valley fold

Folding the paper in the usual way.

Valley and unfold

Make a crease, then unfold it.

Mountain fold

Folding a flap or layer behind. Can usually be made as a valley fold by turning the paper over.

Turn over

Lift the paper up and turn it upside down, like tossing a pancake.

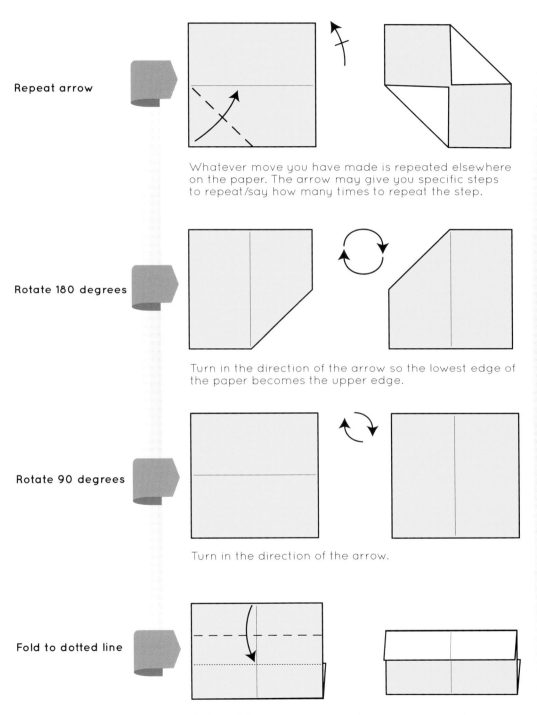

Repeat arrow

Whatever move you have made is repeated elsewhere on the paper. The arrow may give you specific steps to repeat/say how many times to repeat the step.

Rotate 180 degrees

Turn in the direction of the arrow so the lowest edge of the paper becomes the upper edge.

Rotate 90 degrees

Turn in the direction of the arrow.

Fold to dotted line

A dotted line shows an imaginary crease or edge as guidance for a fold.

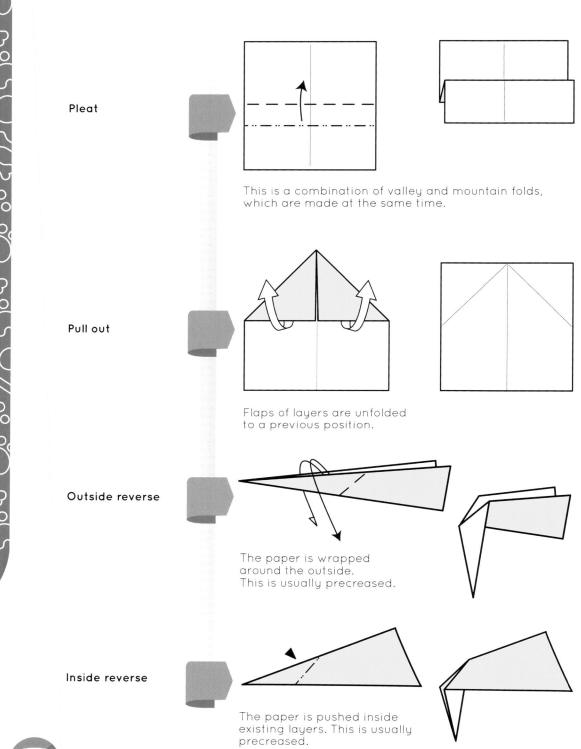

Pleat

This is a combination of valley and mountain folds, which are made at the same time.

Pull out

Flaps of layers are unfolded to a previous position.

Outside reverse

The paper is wrapped around the outside. This is usually precreased.

Inside reverse

The paper is pushed inside existing layers. This is usually precreased.

Double reverse fold

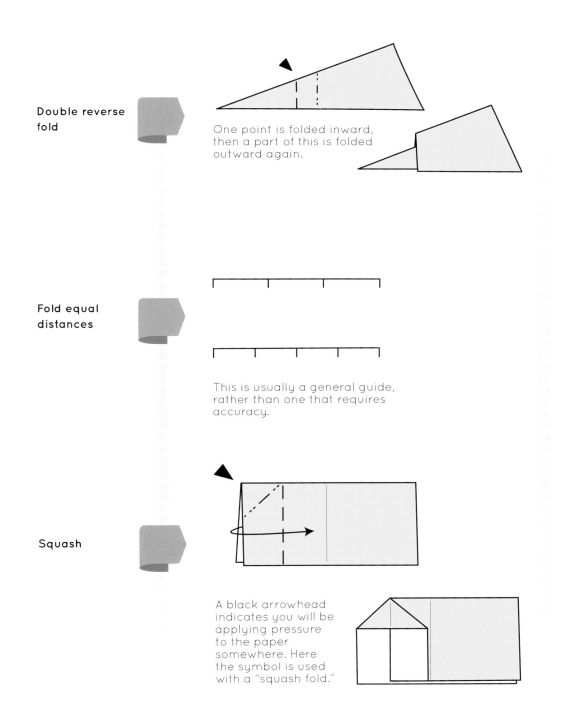

One point is folded inward, then a part of this is folded outward again.

Fold equal distances

This is usually a general guide, rather than one that requires accuracy.

Squash

A black arrowhead indicates you will be applying pressure to the paper somewhere. Here the symbol is used with a "squash fold."

Basic Dog

Traditional

You can easily make lots of variations.
Don't forget to draw the eyes!

Size of the sheet: 7 x 7 in

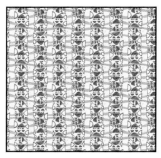

Paper

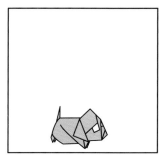

Relationship between
the paper and the origami

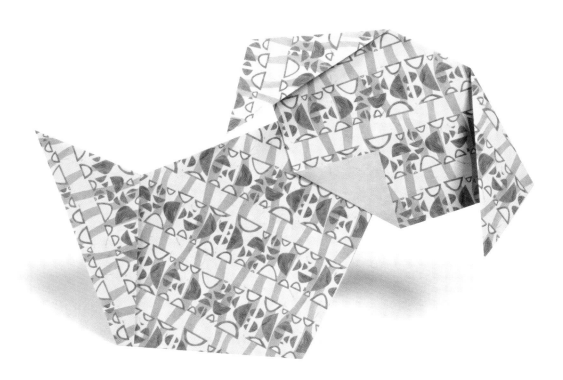

THE HEAD

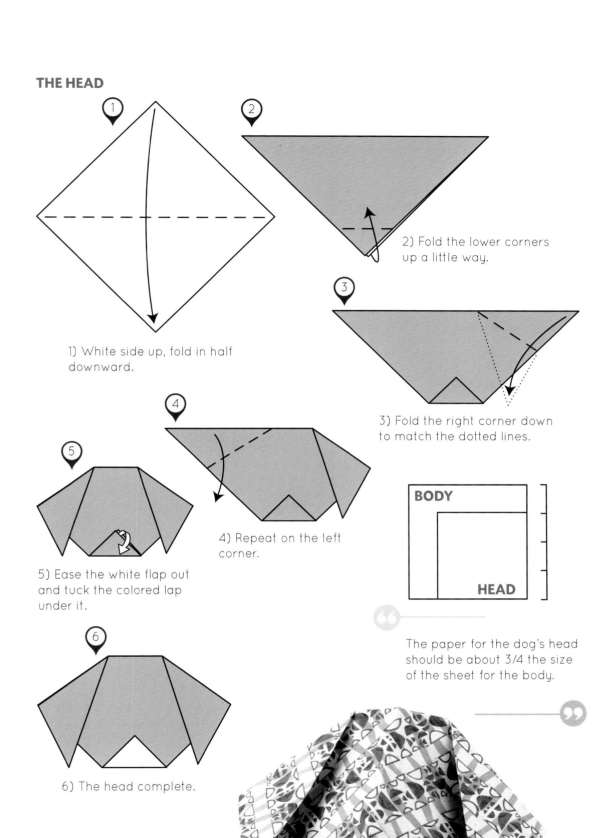

1) White side up, fold in half downward.

2) Fold the lower corners up a little way.

3) Fold the right corner down to match the dotted lines.

4) Repeat on the left corner.

5) Ease the white flap out and tuck the colored lap under it.

6) The head complete.

BODY

HEAD

The paper for the dog's head should be about 3/4 the size of the sheet for the body.

THE BODY

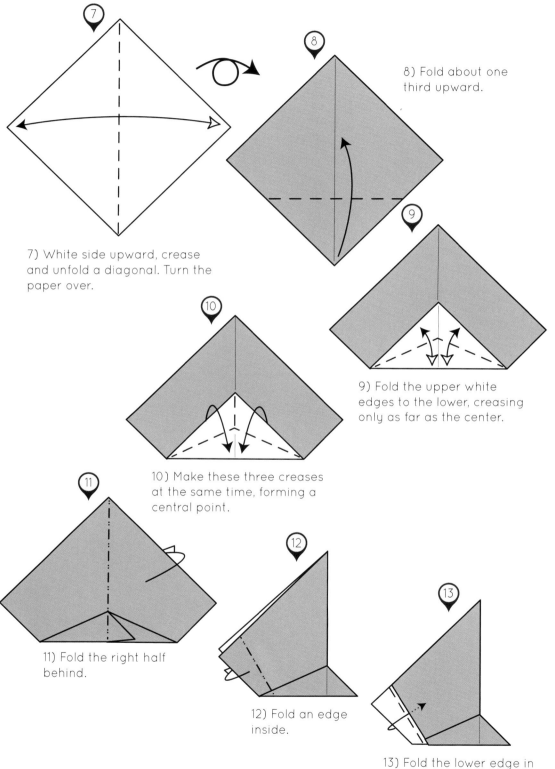

7) White side upward, crease and unfold a diagonal. Turn the paper over.

8) Fold about one third upward.

9) Fold the upper white edges to the lower, creasing only as far as the center.

10) Make these three creases at the same time, forming a central point.

11) Fold the right half behind.

12) Fold an edge inside.

13) Fold the lower edge in as well. Rotate the paper.

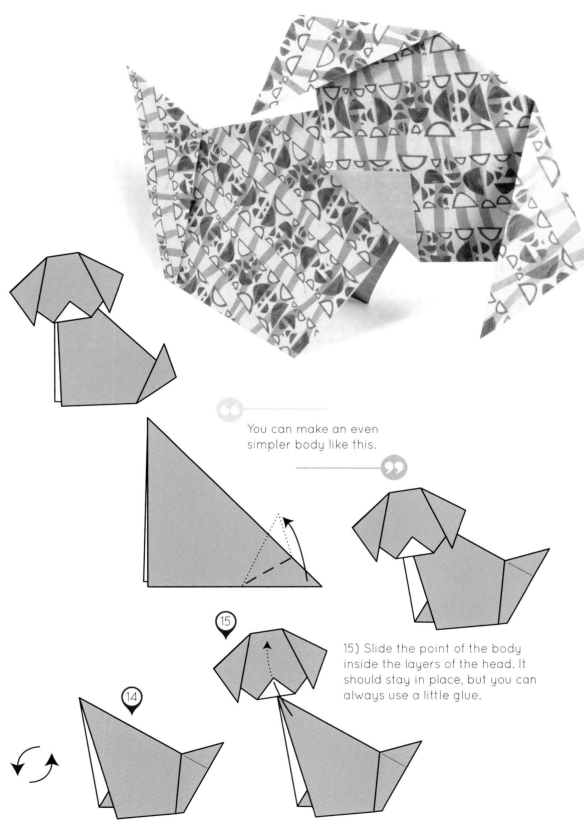

You can make an even simpler body like this.

15) Slide the point of the body inside the layers of the head. It should stay in place, but you can always use a little glue.

14) The body is complete.

Minimal Dog

Nick Robinson

Just a few creases are all you need. Try altering every step to see how it affects the finished model.

Size of the sheet: 7 x 7 in

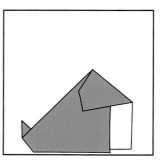

Paper

Relationship between the paper and the origami

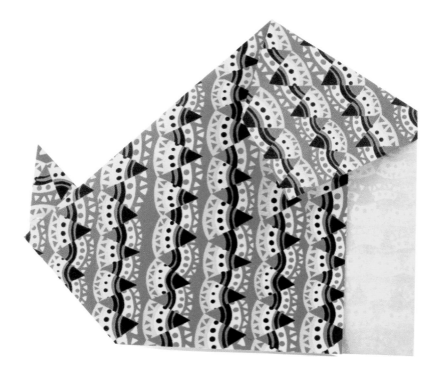

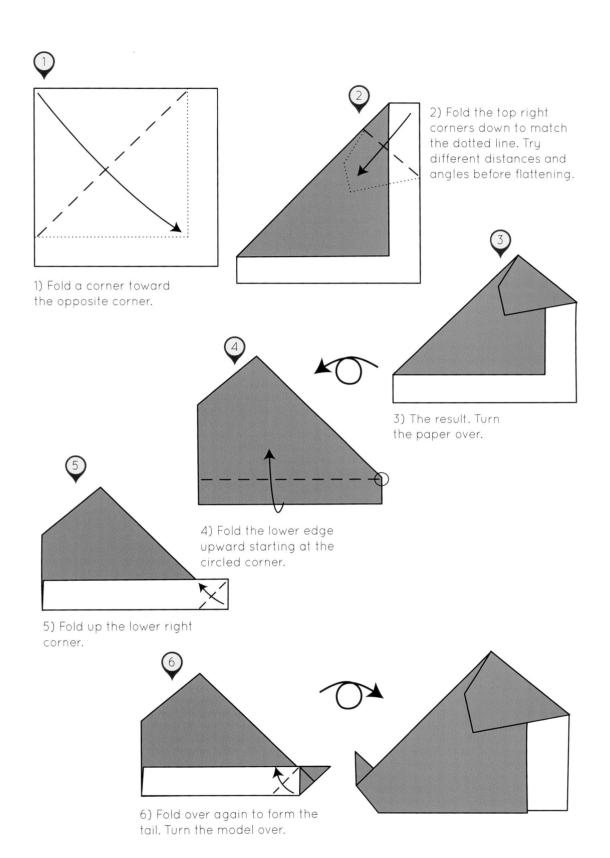

1) Fold a corner toward the opposite corner.

2) Fold the top right corners down to match the dotted line. Try different distances and angles before flattening.

3) The result. Turn the paper over.

4) Fold the lower edge upward starting at the circled corner.

5) Fold up the lower right corner.

6) Fold over again to form the tail. Turn the model over.

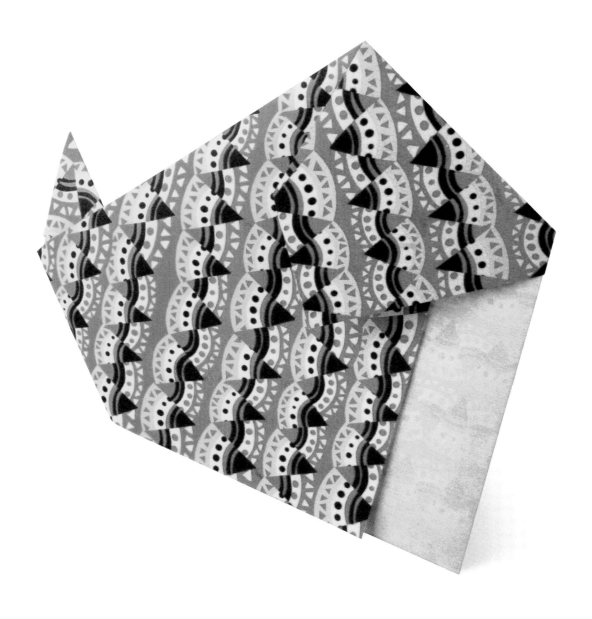

Yoshizawa's Dog

Akira Yoshizawa

Almost every step can be adjusted
to suit your own idea of how the dog should look.

Size of the sheet: 7 x 7 in

Paper

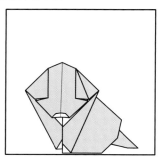

Relationship between
the paper and the origami

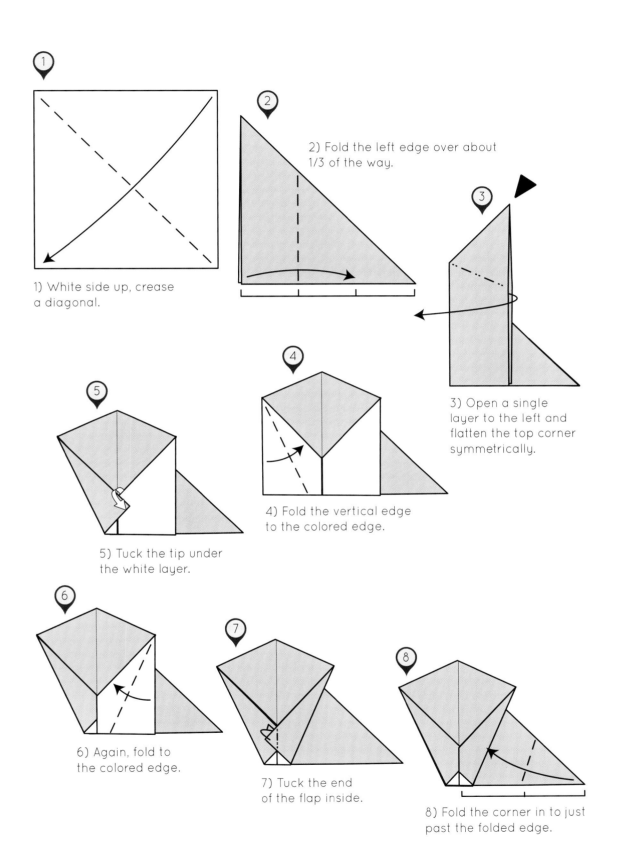

1) White side up, crease a diagonal.

2) Fold the left edge over about 1/3 of the way.

3) Open a single layer to the left and flatten the top corner symmetrically.

4) Fold the vertical edge to the colored edge.

5) Tuck the tip under the white layer.

6) Again, fold to the colored edge.

7) Tuck the end of the flap inside.

8) Fold the corner in to just past the folded edge.

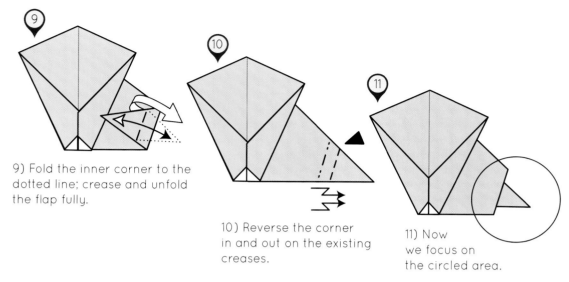

9) Fold the inner corner to the dotted line; crease and unfold the flap fully.

10) Reverse the corner in and out on the existing creases.

11) Now we focus on the circled area.

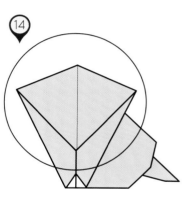

14) Now we focus on the circled area.

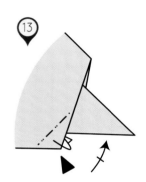

13) Reverse the corner inside. Repeat behind.

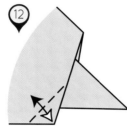

12) Crease firmly, then unfold.

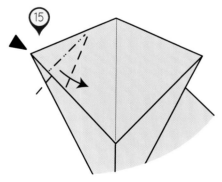

15) Begin to fold the valley on the right, then lift and open the rest of the flap, adjusting into position (see the next drawing) before flattening.

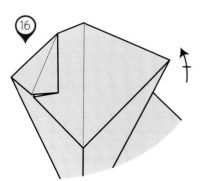

16) Repeat to make the right ear. They can be different if you like!

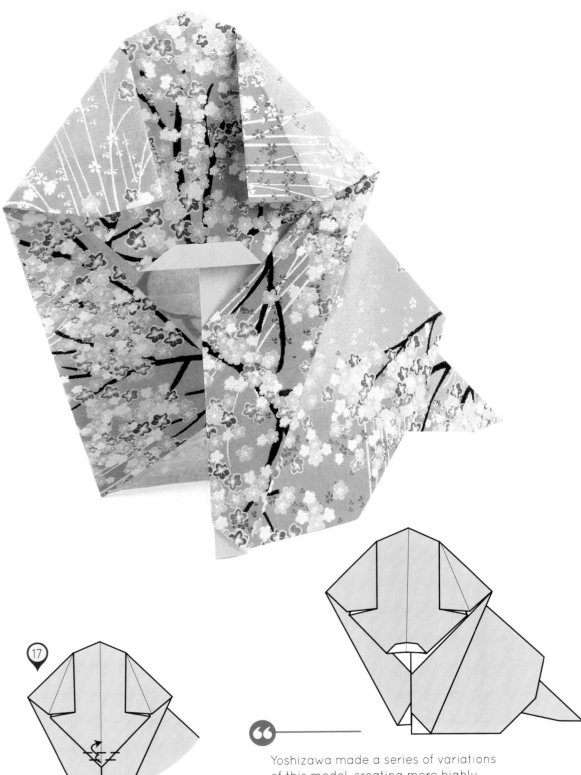

17) Roll the point over twice to form the nose.

Yoshizawa made a series of variations of this model, creating more highly developed eyes and ears. Search on the internet for photos and see if you can recreate these features!

Alison's Dog

Nick Robinson

You can alter steps 4, 9, 12, and 13 to create different breeds of dog.
This was designed for my wife, who wants a dog in the house,
but I feel that two cats are enough!

Size of the sheet: 7 x 7 in

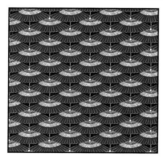

Paper

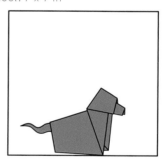

Relationship between
the paper and the origami

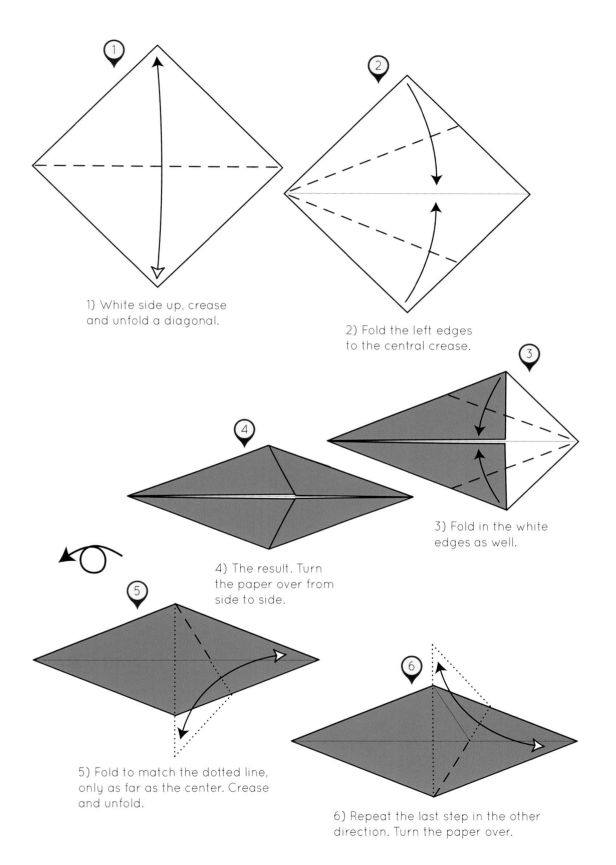

1) White side up, crease and unfold a diagonal.

2) Fold the left edges to the central crease.

3) Fold in the white edges as well.

4) The result. Turn the paper over from side to side.

5) Fold to match the dotted line, only as far as the center. Crease and unfold.

6) Repeat the last step in the other direction. Turn the paper over.

35

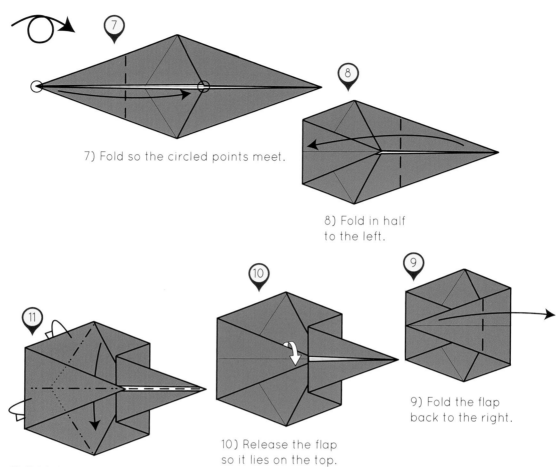

7) Fold so the circled points meet.

8) Fold in half to the left.

9) Fold the flap back to the right.

10) Release the flap so it lies on the top.

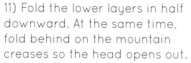

11) Fold the lower layers in half downward. At the same time, fold behind on the mountain creases so the head opens out.

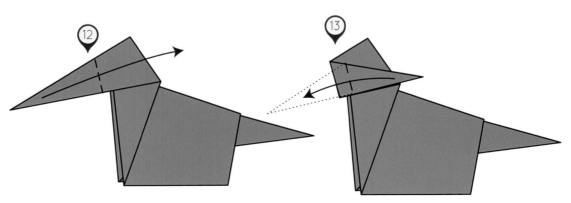

12) Fold the flap to the right. You decide how far and at what angle.

13) Fold the flap to the left. Check how it looks before flattening firmly.

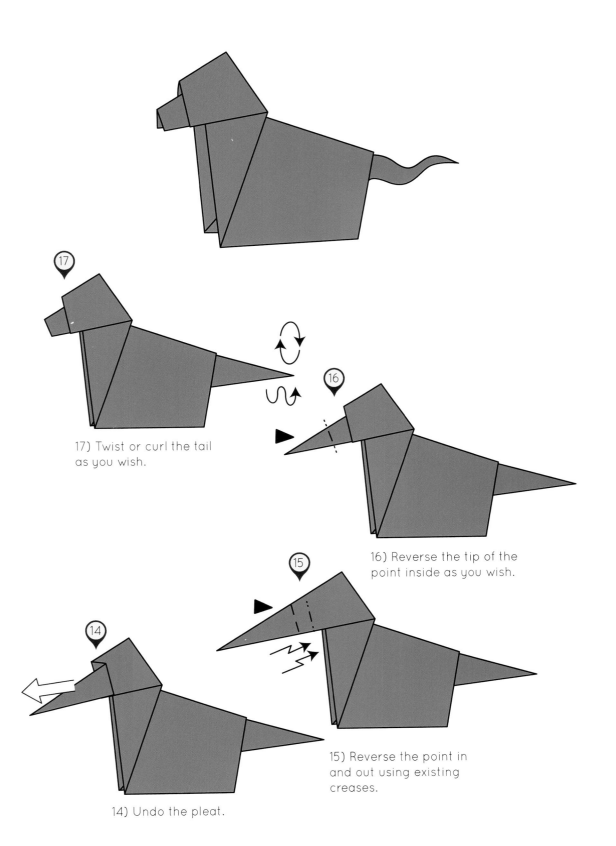

17) Twist or curl the tail as you wish.

16) Reverse the tip of the point inside as you wish.

15) Reverse the point in and out using existing creases.

14) Undo the pleat.

Scotty Dog

Robert Neale

An unusual folding sequence produces a beautiful result.

Size of the sheet: 7 x 7 in

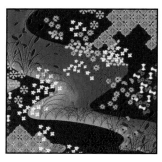

Paper

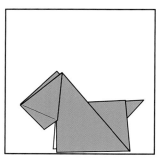

Relationship between
the paper and the origami

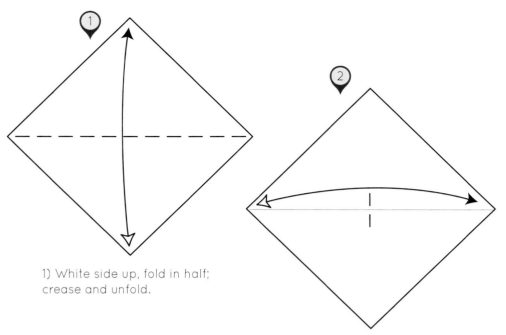

1) White side up, fold in half; crease and unfold.

2) Pinch the center of the diagonal.

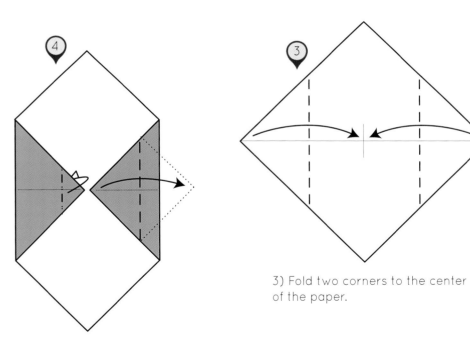

3) Fold two corners to the center of the paper.

4) Fold the right flap outward to match the dotted line and the inner left corner underneath. Neither distance is critical.

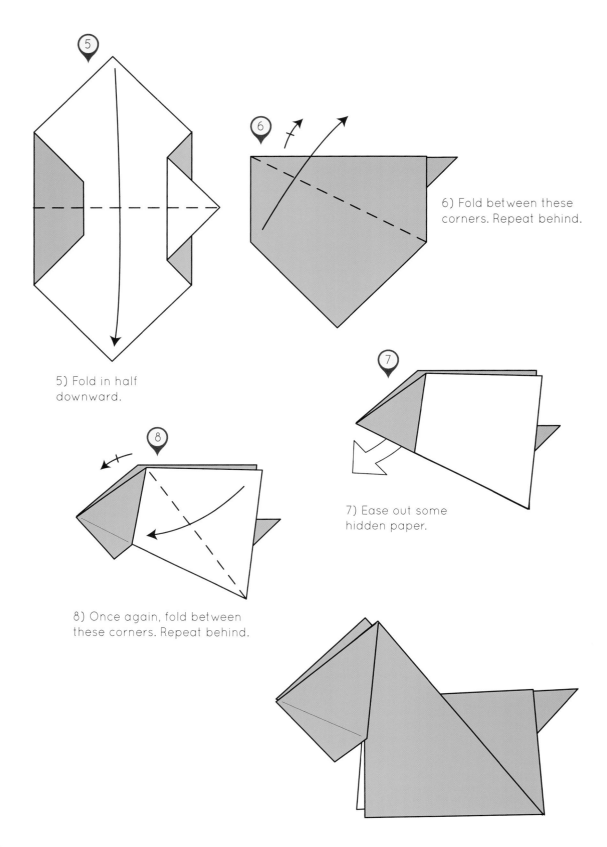

5) Fold in half downward.

6) Fold between these corners. Repeat behind.

7) Ease out some hidden paper.

8) Once again, fold between these corners. Repeat behind.

Gay's Dog

Gay Merrill Gross

Adapted from a fox design by Mitsuo Okuda. You can vary most
of the steps from step 5 onward to produce variations.

Size of the sheet: 7 x 7 in

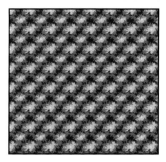

Paper

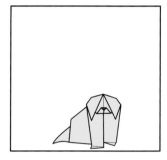

Relationship between
the paper and the origami

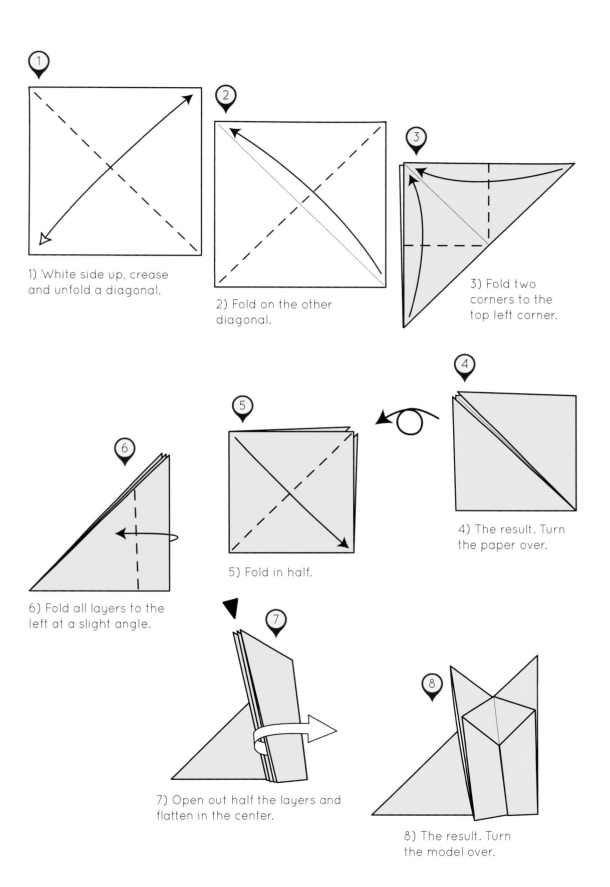

1) White side up, crease and unfold a diagonal.

2) Fold on the other diagonal.

3) Fold two corners to the top left corner.

4) The result. Turn the paper over.

5) Fold in half.

6) Fold all layers to the left at a slight angle.

7) Open out half the layers and flatten in the center.

8) The result. Turn the model over.

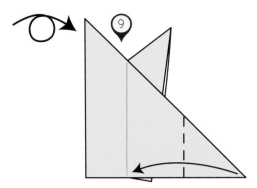

9) Fold the right corner to the left.

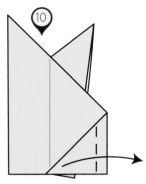

10) Leave a small gap, then fold flap to the right.

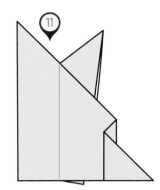

11) The result. Turn the model over.

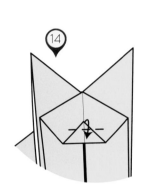

14) Fold the tip down.

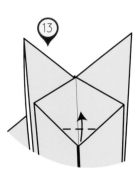

13) Fold up a corner.

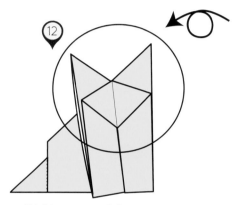

12) Now we will focus on the circled area.

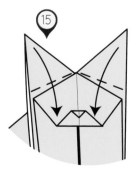

15) Fold the ears down.

16) Fold small corners behind to shape the head.

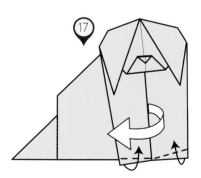

17) Fold up the feet and open the body a little.

Nodding Dog

Nick Robinson

A simple action model—you can make the head nod
or move from side to side!

Size of the sheet: 7 x 7 in

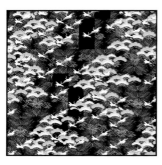

Paper

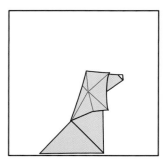

Relationship between
the paper and the origami

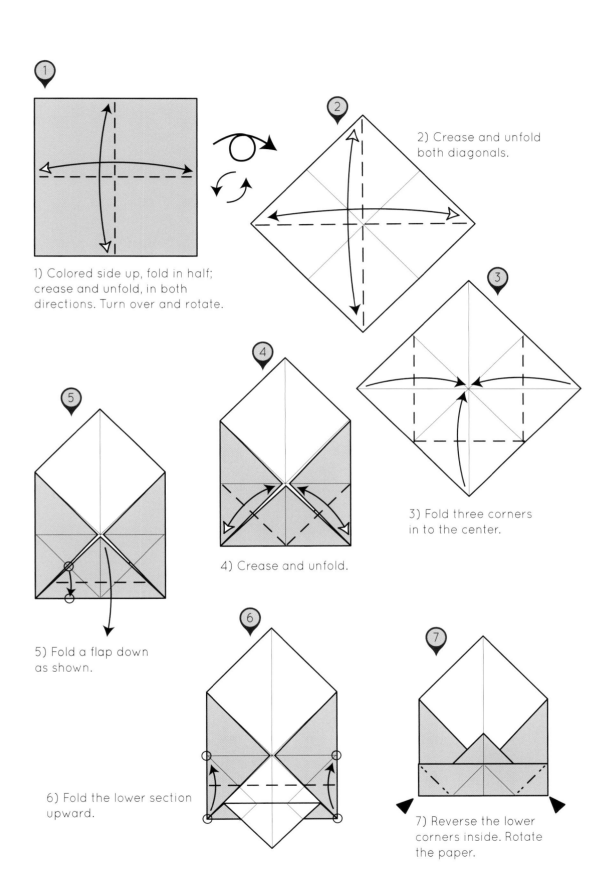

1) Colored side up, fold in half; crease and unfold, in both directions. Turn over and rotate.

2) Crease and unfold both diagonals.

3) Fold three corners in to the center.

4) Crease and unfold.

5) Fold a flap down as shown.

6) Fold the lower section upward.

7) Reverse the lower corners inside. Rotate the paper.

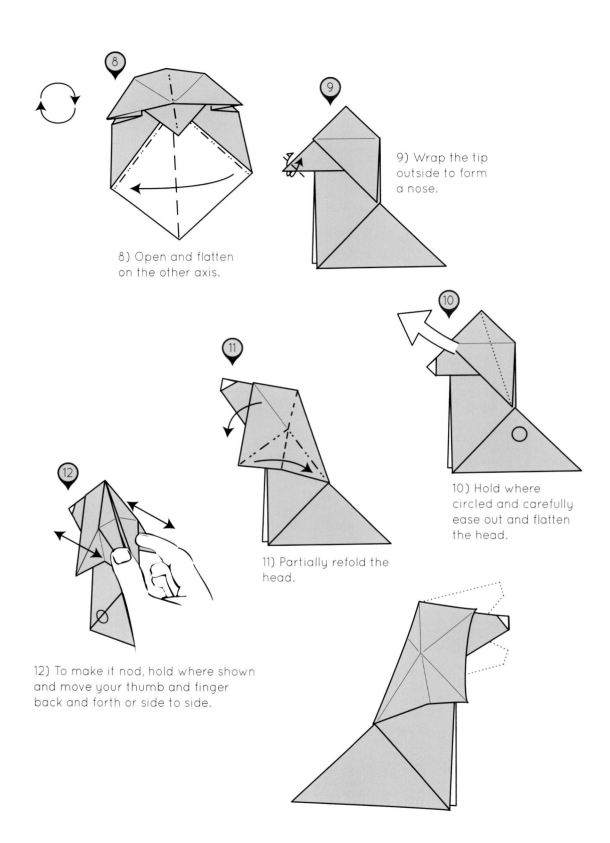

8) Open and flatten on the other axis.

9) Wrap the tip outside to form a nose.

10) Hold where circled and carefully ease out and flatten the head.

11) Partially refold the head.

12) To make it nod, hold where shown and move your thumb and finger back and forth or side to side.

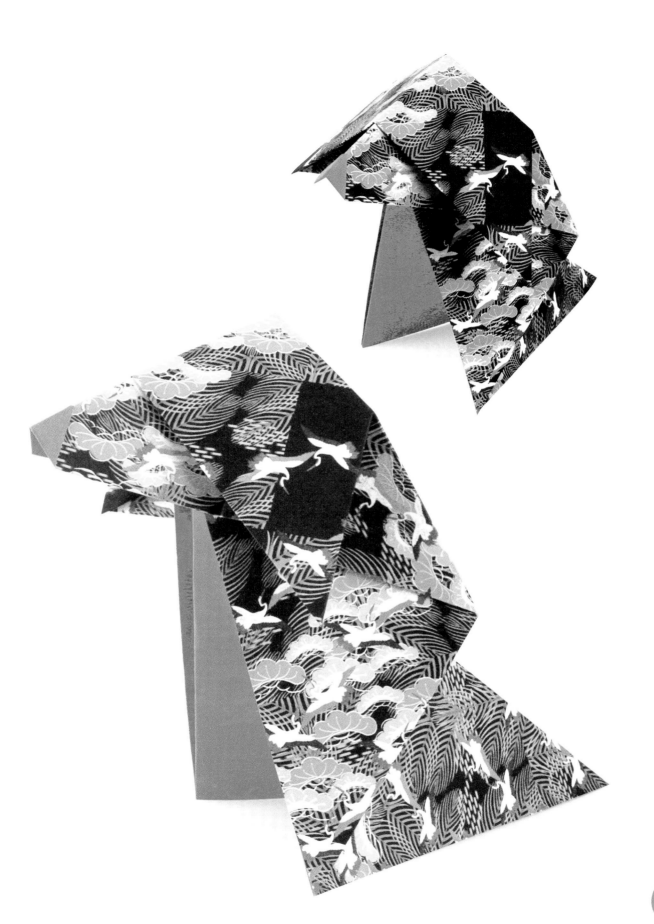

Alsatian

Edwin Corrie

A typically unusual design by this gifted creator.
A square is cut in half to form the front and back of the dog.

Size of the sheet: 7 x 7 in

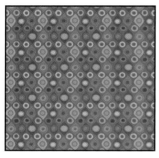

Paper

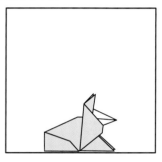

Relationship between
the paper and the origami

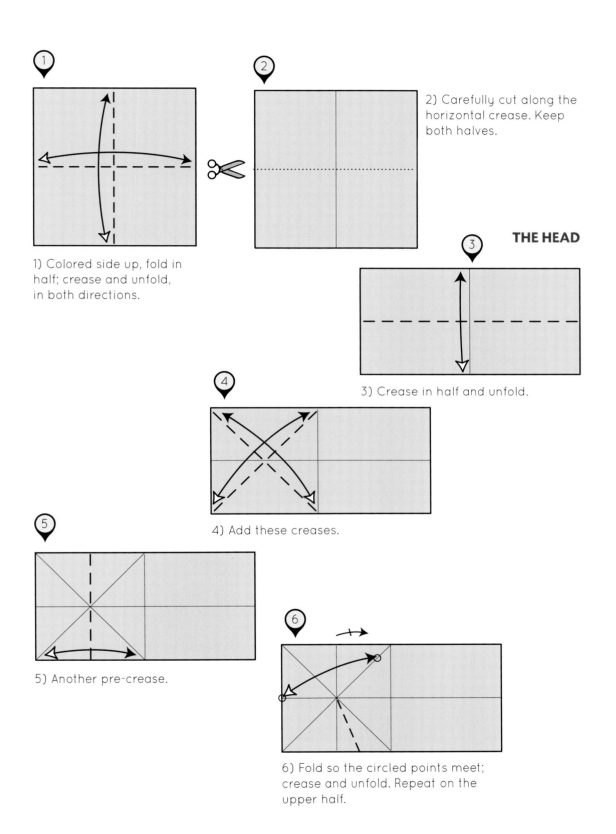

1) Colored side up, fold in half; crease and unfold, in both directions.

2) Carefully cut along the horizontal crease. Keep both halves.

THE HEAD

3) Crease in half and unfold.

4) Add these creases.

5) Another pre-crease.

6) Fold so the circled points meet; crease and unfold. Repeat on the upper half.

53

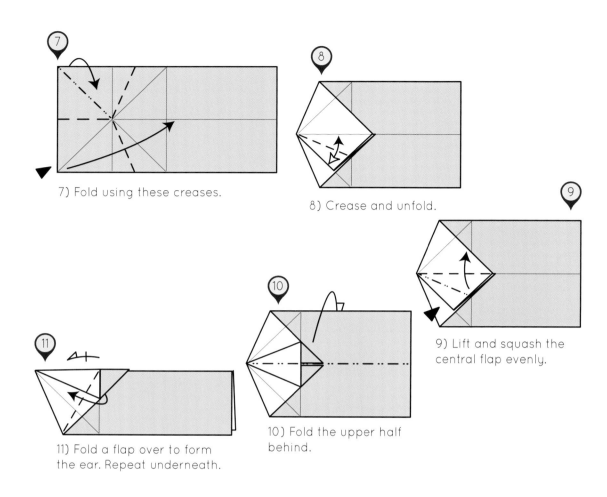

7) Fold using these creases.

8) Crease and unfold.

9) Lift and squash the central flap evenly.

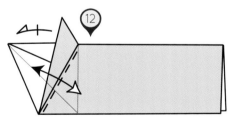

11) Fold a flap over to form the ear. Repeat underneath.

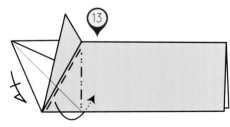

10) Fold the upper half behind.

12) Make this fold through the upper layer only. Repeat underneath.

13) Fold the head section back inside using these creases on both sides.

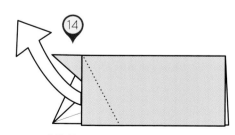

14) Partially open up the paper from inside.

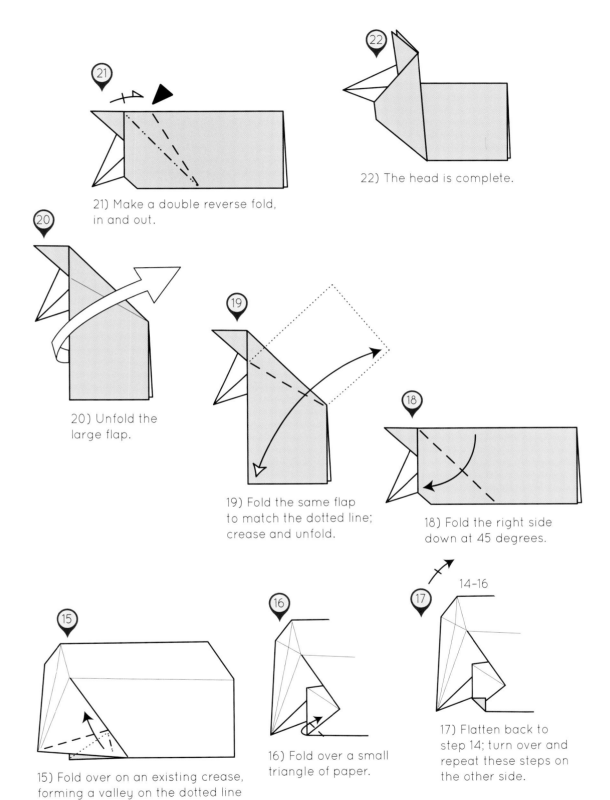

21) Make a double reverse fold, in and out.

22) The head is complete.

20) Unfold the large flap.

19) Fold the same flap to match the dotted line; crease and unfold.

18) Fold the right side down at 45 degrees.

14–16

17) Flatten back to step 14; turn over and repeat these steps on the other side.

15) Fold over on an existing crease, forming a valley on the dotted line and flattening the result.

16) Fold over a small triangle of paper.

THE BODY

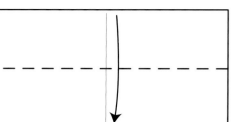

23) Start at step 3 of the head. Fold in half downward.

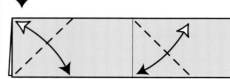

24) Make these creases, then unfold.

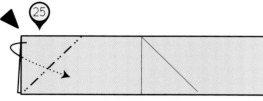

25) Reverse the corner inside.

26) Reverse the flap on the right inside and down.

27) Fold down from the top left corner so the lower edge is horizontal. Make the crease firmly, then unfold.

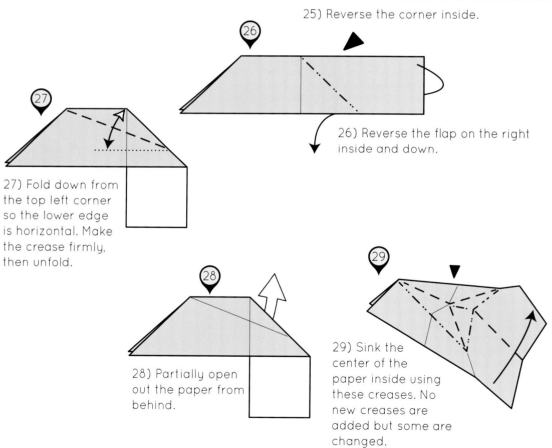

28) Partially open out the paper from behind.

29) Sink the center of the paper inside using these creases. No new creases are added but some are changed.

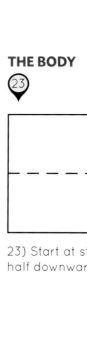

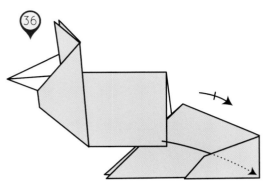

36) Slide both corners of the head section into pockets of the body section.

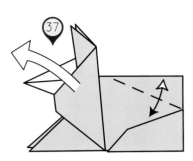

37) Fold over hidden edge; then unfold and separate the sections.

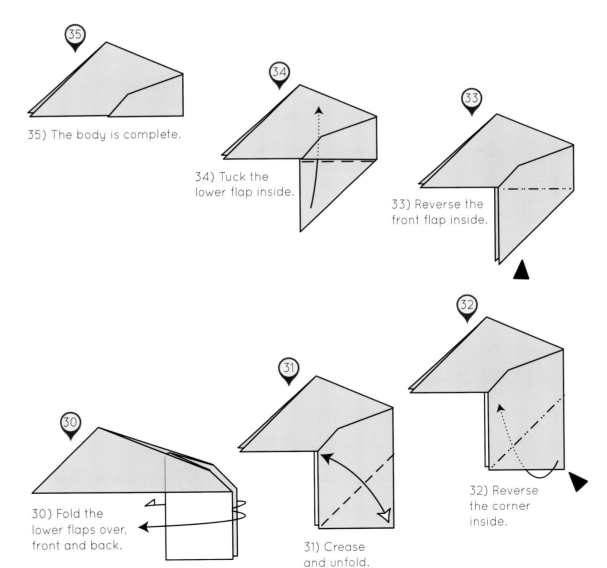

35) The body is complete.

34) Tuck the lower flap inside.

33) Reverse the front flap inside.

32) Reverse the corner inside.

31) Crease and unfold.

30) Fold the lower flaps over, front and back.

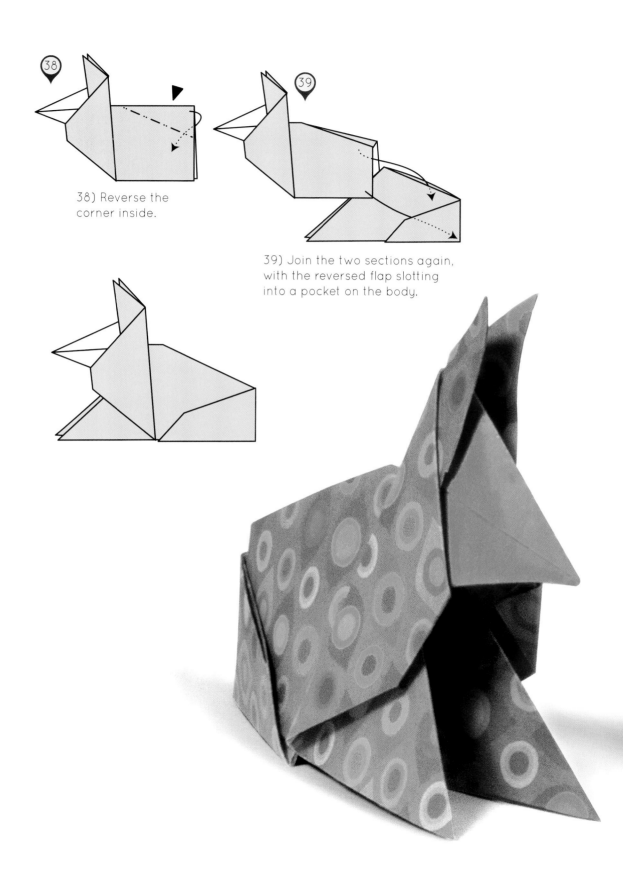

38) Reverse the corner inside.

39) Join the two sections again, with the reversed flap slotting into a pocket on the body.

Kirschenbaum's Dog

Marc Kirschenbaum

A well-engineered approach to the subject
from the New York-based creator. The final model is 3D.

Size of the sheet: 7 x 7 in

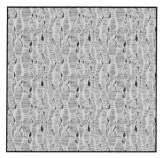

Paper

Relationship between
the paper and the origami

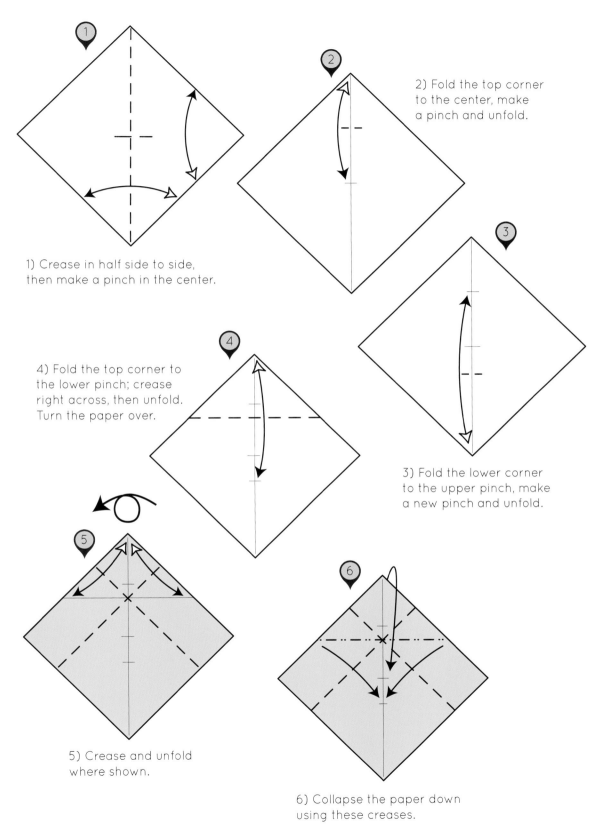

1) Crease in half side to side, then make a pinch in the center.

2) Fold the top corner to the center, make a pinch and unfold.

3) Fold the lower corner to the upper pinch, make a new pinch and unfold.

4) Fold the top corner to the lower pinch; crease right across, then unfold. Turn the paper over.

5) Crease and unfold where shown.

6) Collapse the paper down using these creases.

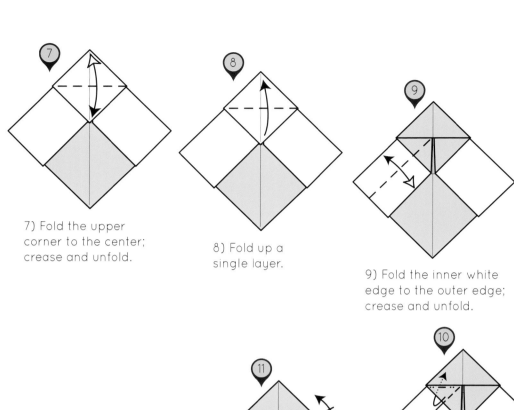

7) Fold the upper corner to the center; crease and unfold.

8) Fold up a single layer.

9) Fold the inner white edge to the outer edge; crease and unfold.

10) Refold the layer, tucking the colored triangle underneath.

11) Repeat steps 9–10 on the right side.

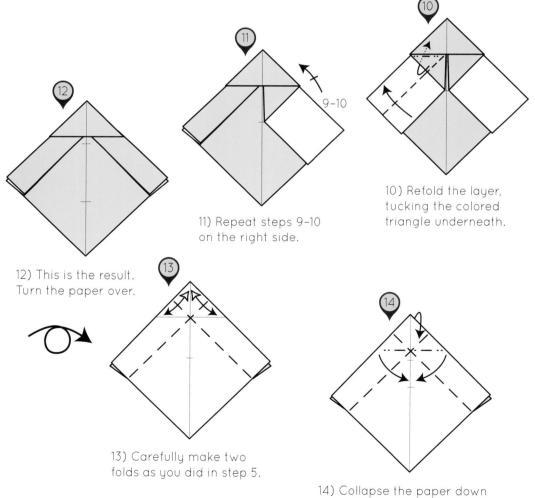

12) This is the result. Turn the paper over.

13) Carefully make two folds as you did in step 5.

14) Collapse the paper down as you did in step 6.

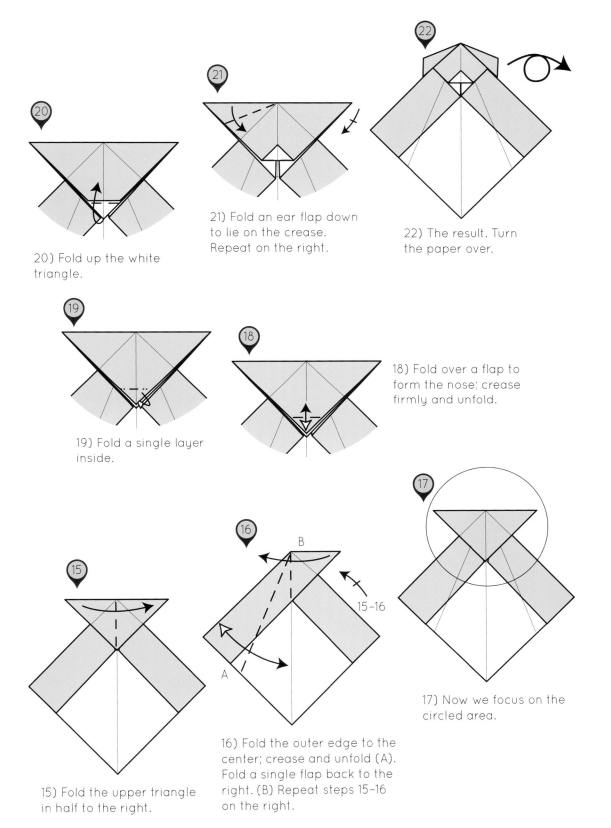

20) Fold up the white triangle.

21) Fold an ear flap down to lie on the crease. Repeat on the right.

22) The result. Turn the paper over.

19) Fold a single layer inside.

18) Fold over a flap to form the nose; crease firmly and unfold.

17) Now we focus on the circled area.

15) Fold the upper triangle in half to the right.

16) Fold the outer edge to the center; crease and unfold (A). Fold a single flap back to the right. (B) Repeat steps 15–16 on the right.

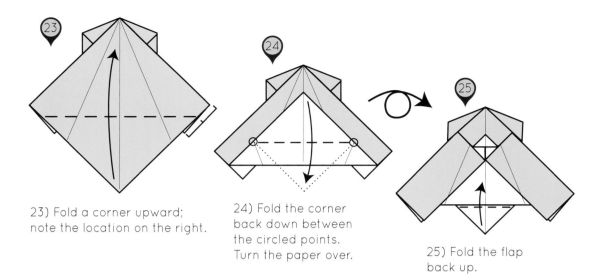

23) Fold a corner upward; note the location on the right.

24) Fold the corner back down between the circled points. Turn the paper over.

25) Fold the flap back up.

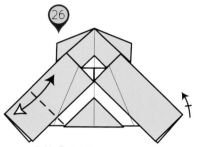

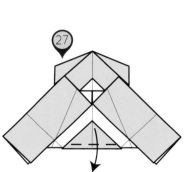

26) Fold through all layers where shown. Repeat on the right.

27) Leave a small gap, then fold the flap down again.

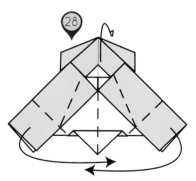

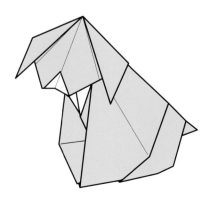

28) Using these creases, form the model into 3D, tucking one leg flap inside the other.

Bone

Nick Robinson

No dog is happy without a bone to chew.
You can use this technique to make bones of any length.

Size of the sheet: 7 x 7 in

Paper

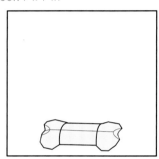

Relationship between
the paper and the origami

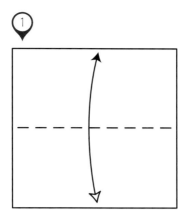

1) White side up, fold in half; crease and unfold.

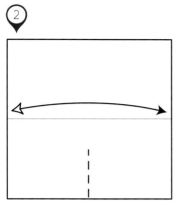

2) Fold in half from side to side, folding about 1/3 of the lower height.

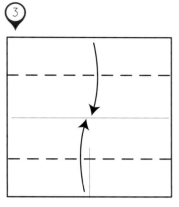

3) Fold upper and lower edges to the center.

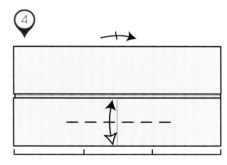

5) Fold in about 1/3 of the way to the center. Repeat on the right.

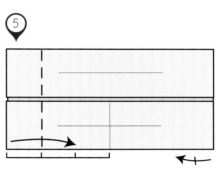

4) Make this crease only where shown. Repeat at the top.

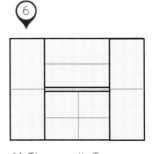

6) The result. Turn the paper over.

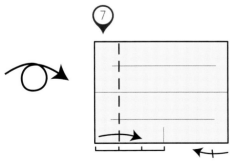

7) Fold in about 1/3 of the way to the center, allowing a flap to flip out from underneath. Repeat on the right.

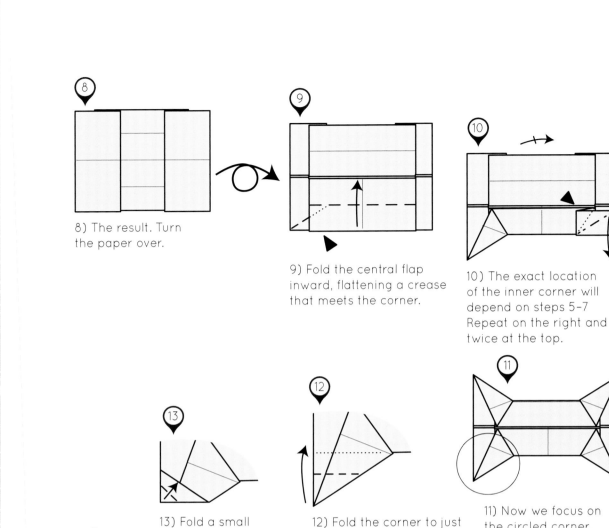

8) The result. Turn the paper over.

9) Fold the central flap inward, flattening a crease that meets the corner.

10) The exact location of the inner corner will depend on steps 5–7 Repeat on the right and twice at the top.

11) Now we focus on the circled corner.

13) Fold a small corner over.

12) Fold the corner to just past the dotted line.

14) Advanced folders may wish to tuck the lower flap inside with a mountain fold, but skip this step if you wish.

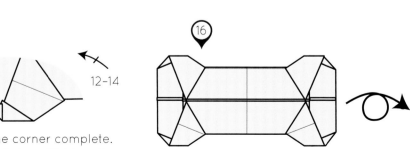

12–14

15) The corner complete. Repeat steps 12–14 on the other corners.

16) The result. Turn the model over.

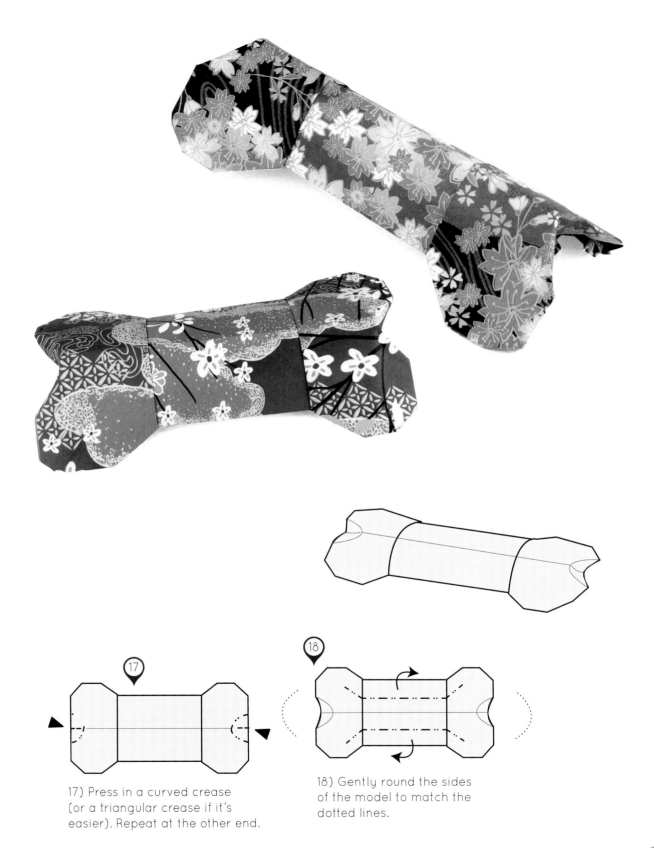

17) Press in a curved crease (or a triangular crease if it's easier). Repeat at the other end.

18) Gently round the sides of the model to match the dotted lines.

Dog

Shoko Aoyagi

A beautifully surprising model, where the dog is revealed
at the very end of the sequence.

Size of the sheet: 7 x 7 in

Paper

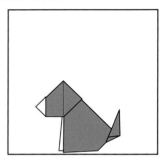

Relationship between
the paper and the origami

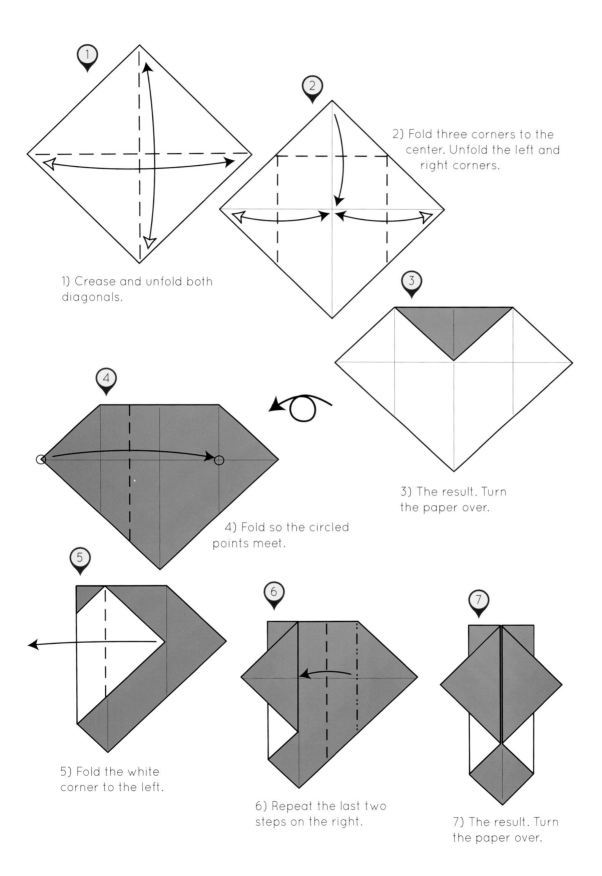

1) Crease and unfold both diagonals.

2) Fold three corners to the center. Unfold the left and right corners.

3) The result. Turn the paper over.

4) Fold so the circled points meet.

5) Fold the white corner to the left.

6) Repeat the last two steps on the right.

7) The result. Turn the paper over.

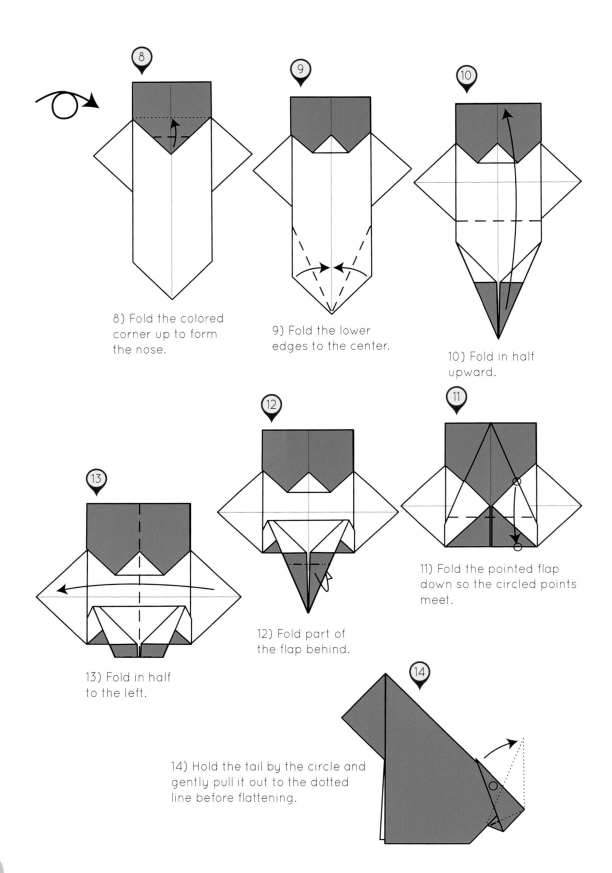

8) Fold the colored corner up to form the nose.

9) Fold the lower edges to the center.

10) Fold in half upward.

11) Fold the pointed flap down so the circled points meet.

12) Fold part of the flap behind.

13) Fold in half to the left.

14) Hold the tail by the circle and gently pull it out to the dotted line before flattening.

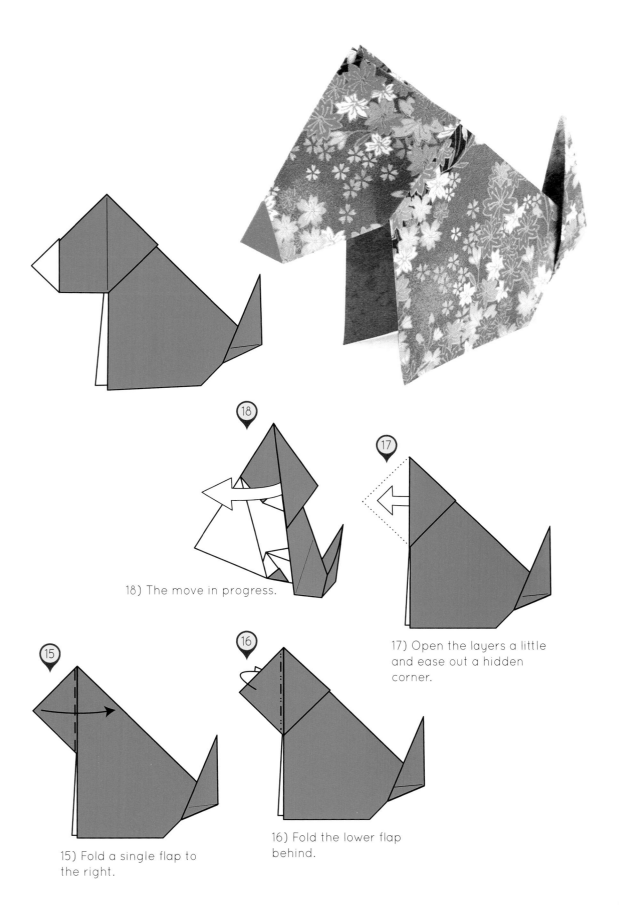

18) The move in progress.

17) Open the layers a little and ease out a hidden corner.

15) Fold a single flap to the right.

16) Fold the lower flap behind.

Puppy

Shoko Aoyagi

Two sheets of paper are needed. The paper for the head should be around 2/3 the size of that for the body, or perhaps a little smaller. Experiment!

Size of the sheet: 7 x 7 in

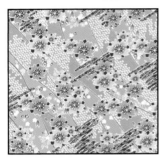

Paper

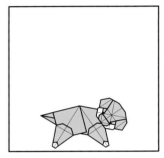

Relationship between
the paper and the origami

THE HEAD

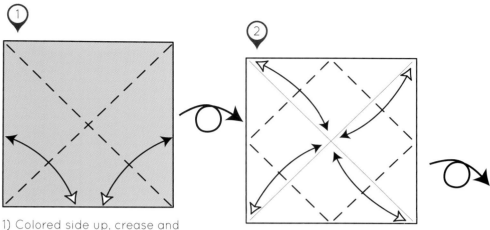

1) Colored side up, crease and unfold both diagonals. Turn the paper over.

2) Fold all corners to the center, then unfold. Turn the paper over.

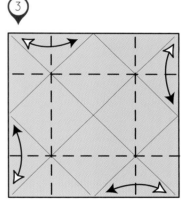

3) Fold each edge to the center; crease and unfold.

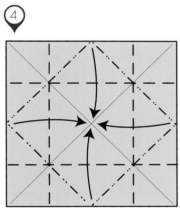

4) Fold the center of each edge to the center of the paper using these creases.

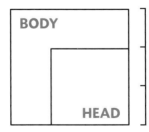

❝ The paper for the dog's head should be about 2/3 the size of the sheet for the body. ❞

BODY

HEAD

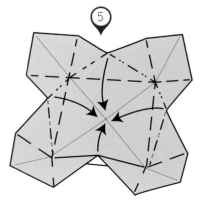

5) The fold in progress.

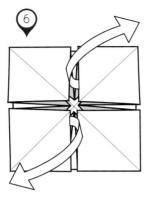

6) Unfold back to the square and turn to the white side.

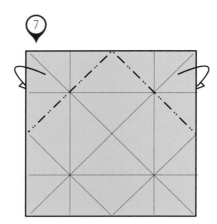

7) Fold the upper corners underneath.

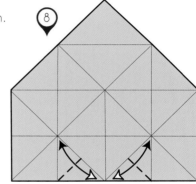

8) Make two small pre-creases.

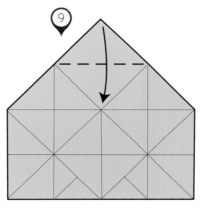

9) Fold the upper corner to the center.

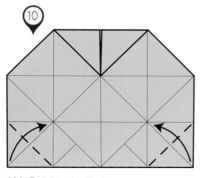

10) Fold in both lower corners.

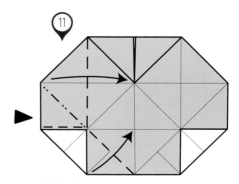

11) Valley the lower crease; reverse the upper corner inside.

76

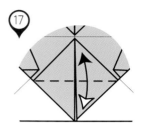

17) Crease and unfold.

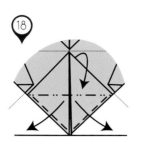

18) Open the inner edges, flattening downward.

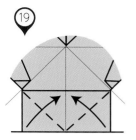

19) Fold in two corners.

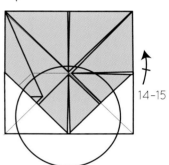

16) Repeat on the right. Now we focus on the circled area.

14-15

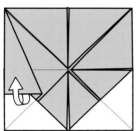

15) Tuck the flap under a layer.

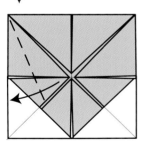

14) Fold an inner edge to the outer edge.

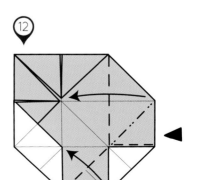

12) Repeat the last step on the right.

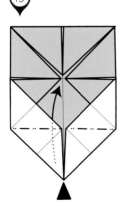

13) Reverse the lower corner inside.

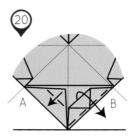

20) Fold the triangle in half (A). Fold the flap over (B).

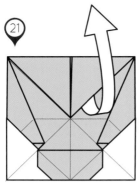

21) Lift up a flap and turn the paper over.

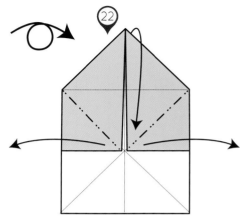

22) Open the corners, flattening the top point down.

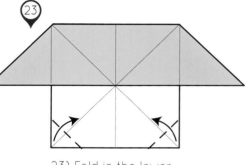

23) Fold in the lower corners.

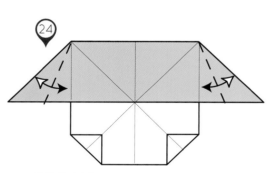

24) Fold the outer edge to the vertical edge; crease and unfold. Repeat on the right. Turn the paper over.

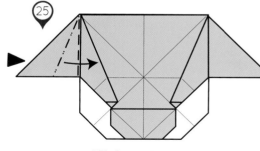

25) Squash the flap open.

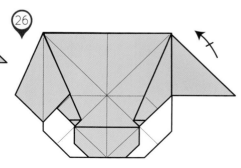

26) Repeat the last step on the right.

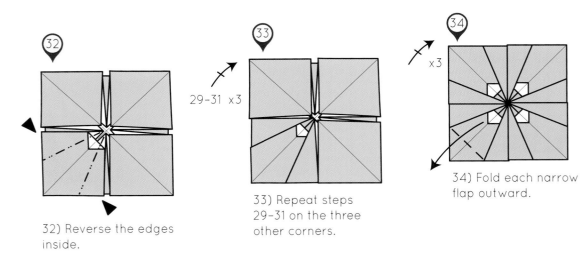

32) Reverse the edges inside.

33) Repeat steps 29–31 on the three other corners.

29–31 x3

x3

34) Fold each narrow flap outward.

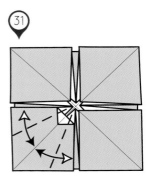

31) Fold the inner edges of the square to the diagonal; crease and unfold.

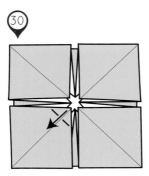

30) Fold a small corner outward.

THE BODY

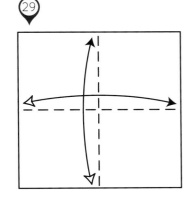

29) For the body, add these creases, then fold to step 6 of the head, starting with the white side upward.

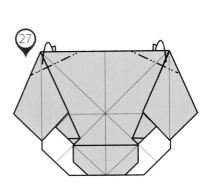

27) Fold two corners behind as you wish.

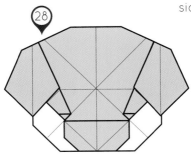

28) The head is complete.

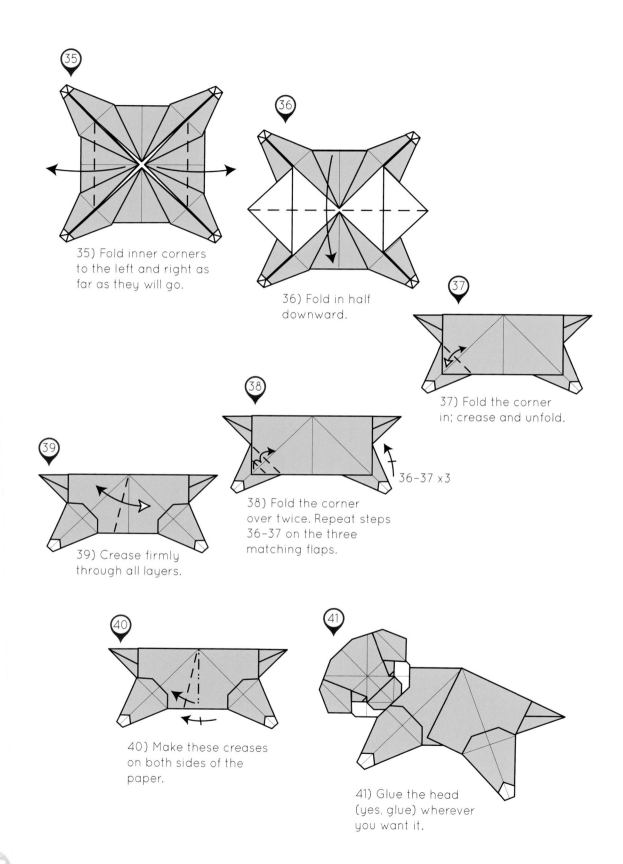

35) Fold inner corners to the left and right as far as they will go.

36) Fold in half downward.

37) Fold the corner in; crease and unfold.

38) Fold the corner over twice. Repeat steps 36–37 on the three matching flaps.

36–37 x3

39) Crease firmly through all layers.

40) Make these creases on both sides of the paper.

41) Glue the head (yes, glue) wherever you want it.

Dawg

Tony O'Hare

A simple dog, but with lots of character.
Try altering angles and distances in steps 5, 11, 19, and 20
to see how you can create variations of your own!

Size of the sheet: 7 x 7 in

Paper

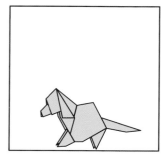

Relationship between
the paper and the origami

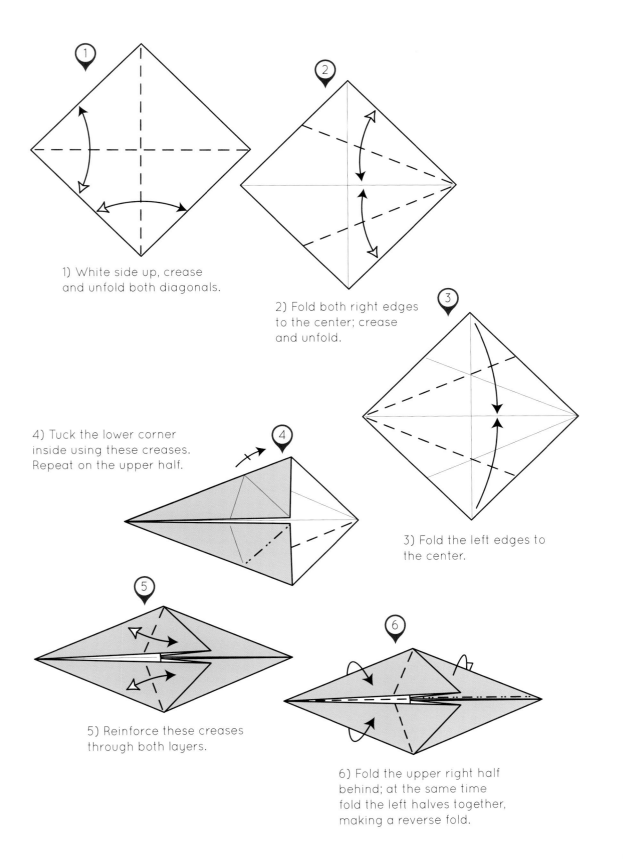

1) White side up, crease and unfold both diagonals.

2) Fold both right edges to the center; crease and unfold.

3) Fold the left edges to the center.

4) Tuck the lower corner inside using these creases. Repeat on the upper half.

5) Reinforce these creases through both layers.

6) Fold the upper right half behind; at the same time fold the left halves together, making a reverse fold.

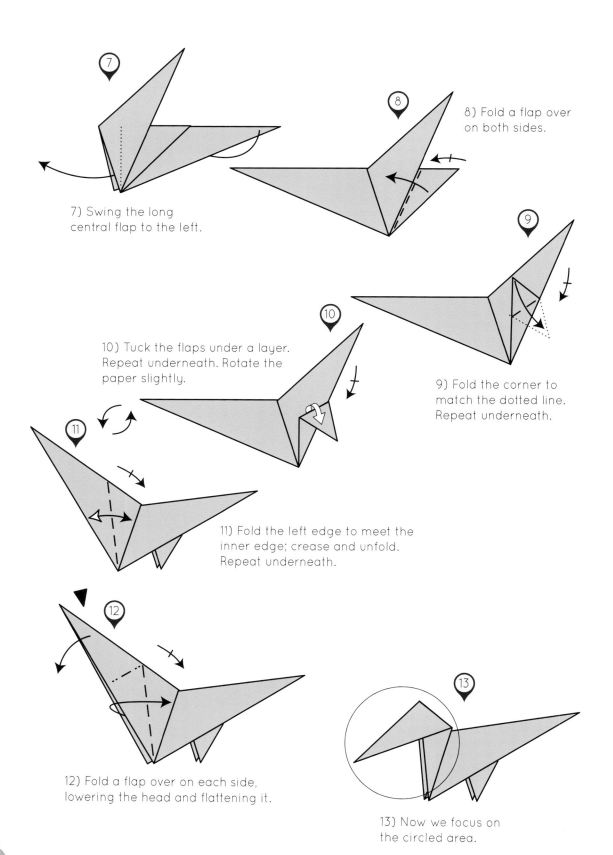

7) Swing the long central flap to the left.

8) Fold a flap over on both sides.

9) Fold the corner to match the dotted line. Repeat underneath.

10) Tuck the flaps under a layer. Repeat underneath. Rotate the paper slightly.

11) Fold the left edge to meet the inner edge; crease and unfold. Repeat underneath.

12) Fold a flap over on each side, lowering the head and flattening it.

13) Now we focus on the circled area.

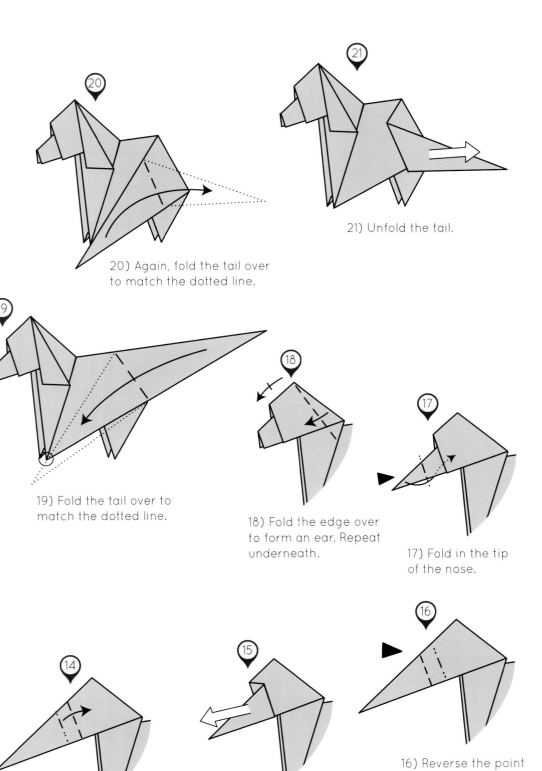

20) Again, fold the tail over to match the dotted line.

21) Unfold the tail.

19) Fold the tail over to match the dotted line.

18) Fold the edge over to form an ear. Repeat underneath.

17) Fold in the tip of the nose.

16) Reverse the point inside and back out.

15) Unfold the pleat.

14) Make a pleat in the paper.

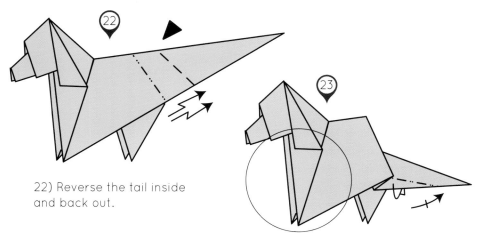

22) Reverse the tail inside and back out.

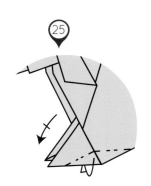

23) Fold part of the tail inside. Repeat underneath. Now focus on the circled area.

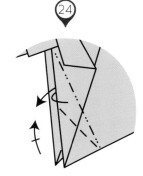

24) Fold the front legs in and out. Repeat underneath.

25) Gently fold on these creases to shape the leg. Repeat underneath.

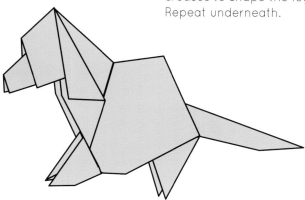

Dog in a Kennel

Nick Robinson

Two sheets of paper are needed for this hound and his home.

Size of the sheet: 7 x 7 in

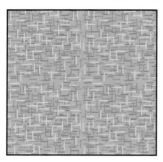

Paper

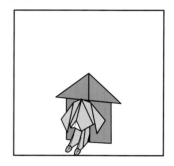

Relationship between
the paper and the origami

THE KENNEL

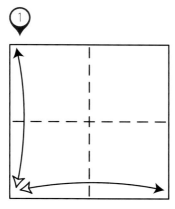

1) Fold in half; crease and unfold in both directions.

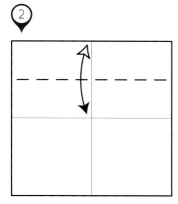

2) Fold the upper edge to the center, then unfold.

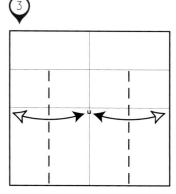

3) Fold the sides to the center, but leave a tiny gap. Crease where shown, then unfold.

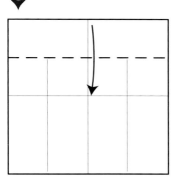

5) Fold in two corners.

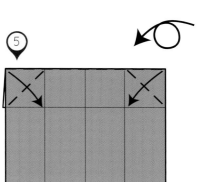

4) Refold the edge to the center and turn the paper over.

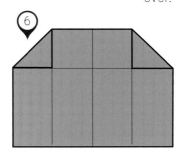

6) The result. Turn the paper over.

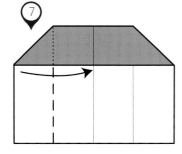

7) Fold the white flap inward.

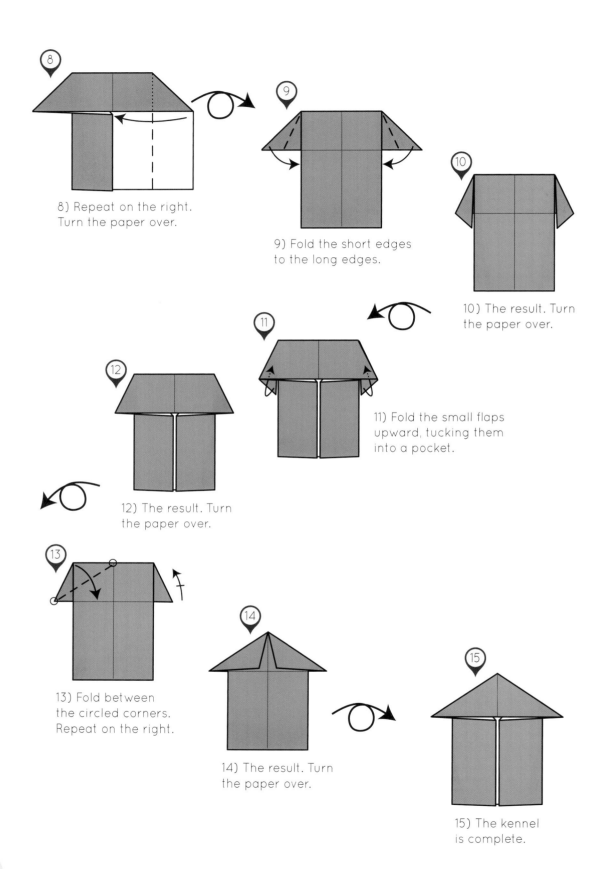

8) Repeat on the right. Turn the paper over.

9) Fold the short edges to the long edges.

10) The result. Turn the paper over.

11) Fold the small flaps upward, tucking them into a pocket.

12) The result. Turn the paper over.

13) Fold between the circled corners. Repeat on the right.

14) The result. Turn the paper over.

15) The kennel is complete.

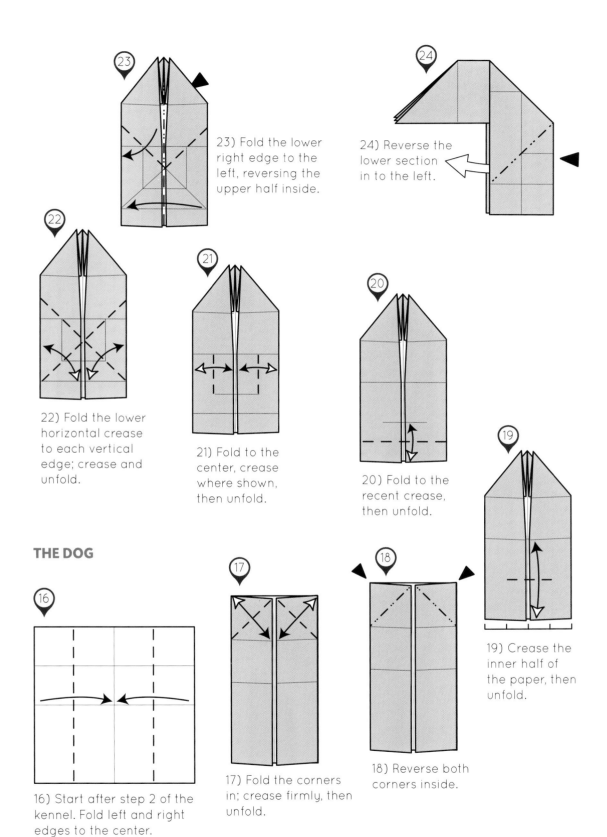

23) Fold the lower right edge to the left, reversing the upper half inside.

24) Reverse the lower section in to the left.

22) Fold the lower horizontal crease to each vertical edge; crease and unfold.

21) Fold to the center, crease where shown, then unfold.

20) Fold to the recent crease, then unfold.

19) Crease the inner half of the paper, then unfold.

THE DOG

16) Start after step 2 of the kennel. Fold left and right edges to the center.

17) Fold the corners in; crease firmly, then unfold.

18) Reverse both corners inside.

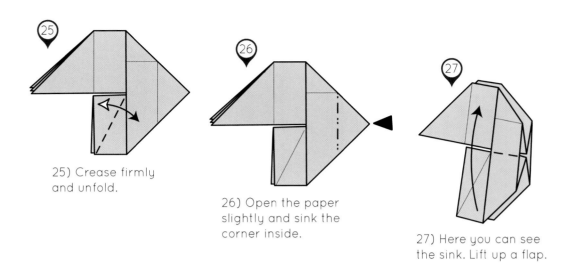

25) Crease firmly and unfold.

26) Open the paper slightly and sink the corner inside.

27) Here you can see the sink. Lift up a flap.

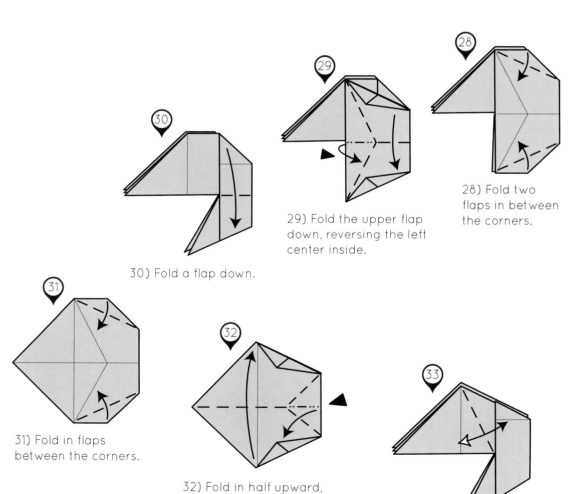

30) Fold a flap down.

29) Fold the upper flap down, reversing the left center inside.

28) Fold two flaps in between the corners.

31) Fold in flaps between the corners.

32) Fold in half upward, reversing in the center of the right edge.

33) Crease and unfold through all layers.

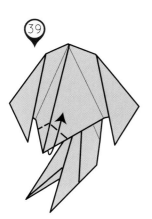

39) Fold over a flap to form the nose. You decide how big it is!

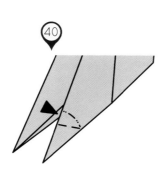

40) Gently squash open the right flap with a curved crease to create a paw.

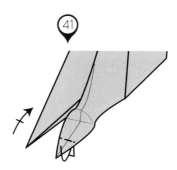

41) Fold the tip underneath. Repeat on the other foot.

38) The arrangement of layers. The central flap may fold to either side. Repeat underneath.

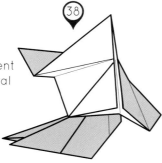

37) Open the head slightly on an existing crease. The internal layers are not symmetrical. The next view is from below.

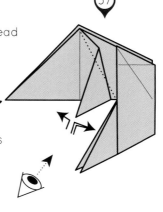

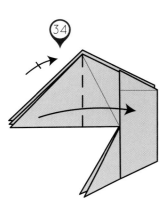

34) Fold a flap to the right. Repeat underneath.

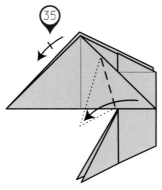

35) Fold a corner to match the dotted line. Repeat underneath. This is the ear, try other positions!

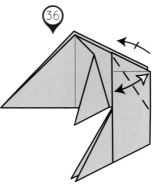

36) Crease and unfold. Repeat underneath.

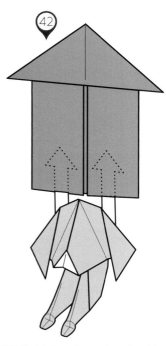

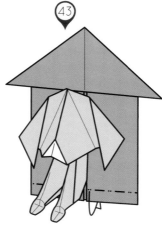

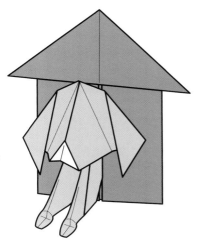

43) Fold the flap underneath on a level with the feet.

42) Fold the flaps level with the feet made in step 21 at 90 degrees, then slide them into the pockets of the kennel.

Woof! Woof! Puppy

Gay Merrill Gross

Based on a design by Nick Robinson. An interesting use
of two squares to make a dog with a nodding head.

Size of the sheet: 7 x 7 in

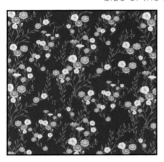

Paper

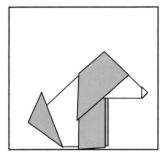

Relationship between
the paper and the origami

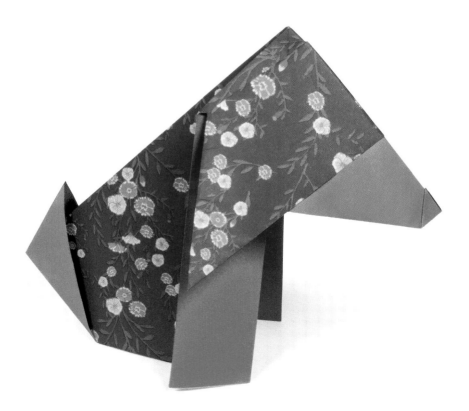

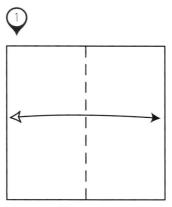

1) Crease and unfold.

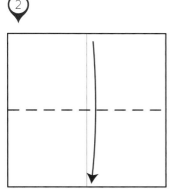

2) Fold in half downward.

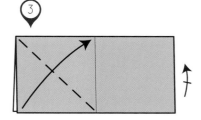

3) Fold a corner to the top edge. Repeat on the right.

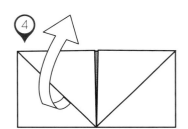

6) Fold over again.

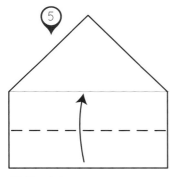

5) Fold the lower section in half.

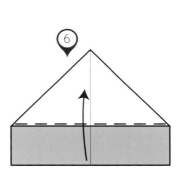

4) Lift the first flap upward.

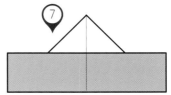

7) The result. Turn the paper over.

8) Fold a corner in half. Repeat on the right.

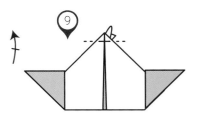

9) Fold the tip behind to form a nose.

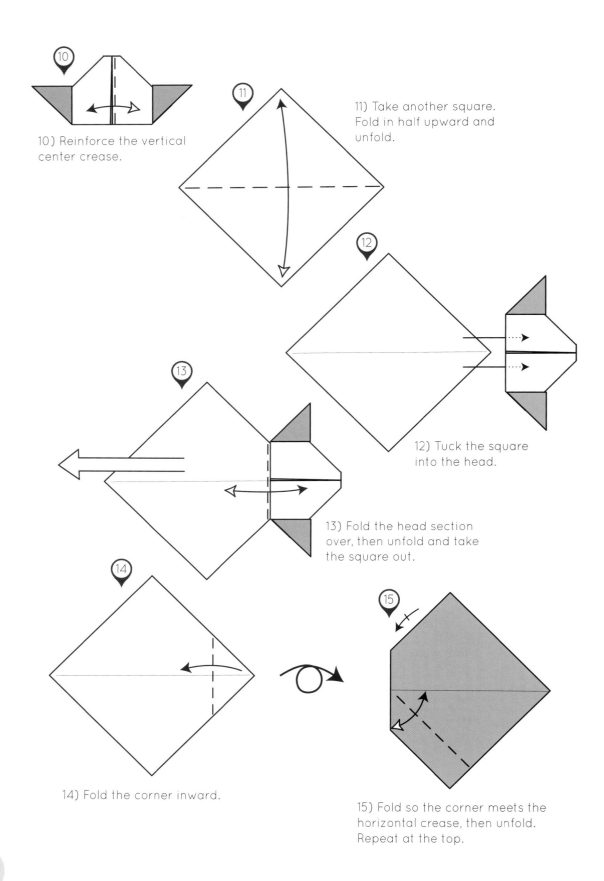

10) Reinforce the vertical center crease.

11) Take another square. Fold in half upward and unfold.

12) Tuck the square into the head.

13) Fold the head section over, then unfold and take the square out.

14) Fold the corner inward.

15) Fold so the corner meets the horizontal crease, then unfold. Repeat at the top.

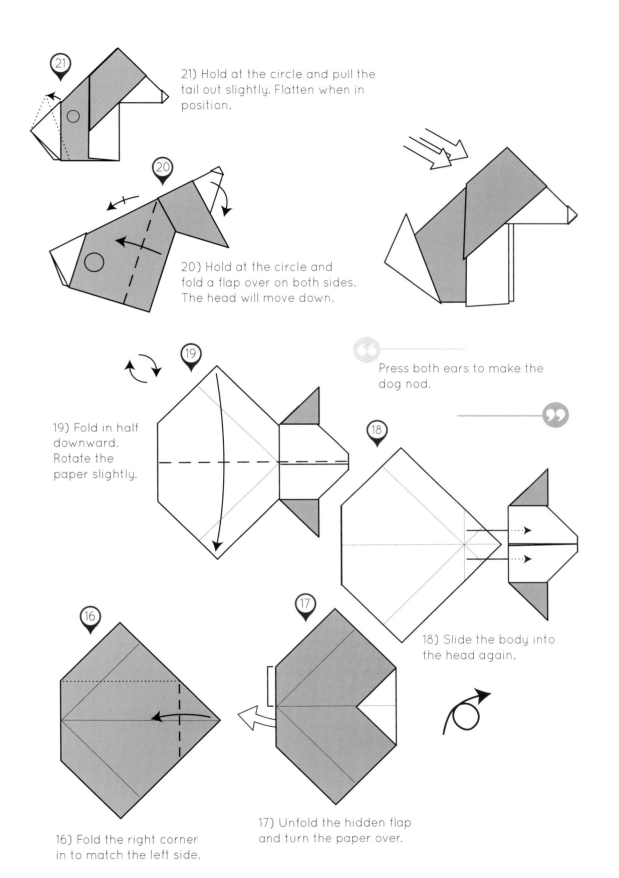

21) Hold at the circle and pull the tail out slightly. Flatten when in position.

20) Hold at the circle and fold a flap over on both sides. The head will move down.

Press both ears to make the dog nod.

19) Fold in half downward. Rotate the paper slightly.

18) Slide the body into the head again.

16) Fold the right corner in to match the left side.

17) Unfold the hidden flap and turn the paper over.

Bodo's Dog

Bodo Haag

Concentrate on folding accurately and you should have no problems completing this model. Do not use thick paper!

Size of the sheet: 7 x 7 in

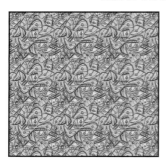

Paper

Relationship between
the paper and the origami

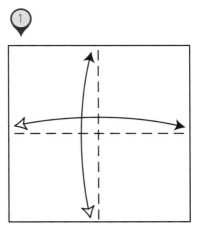

1) White side up, fold in half; crease and unfold, in both directions.

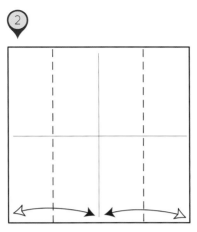

2) Fold left and right edges to the center; crease and unfold.

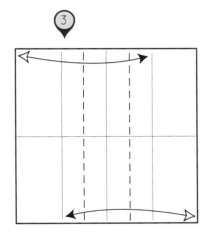

3) Add 3/8 creases.

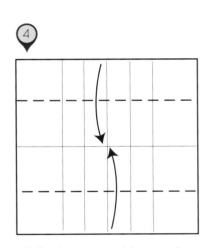

4) Fold upper and lower edges to the center.

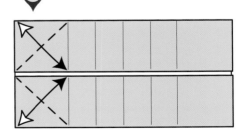

5) Crease and unfold.

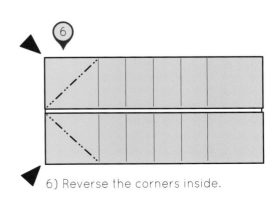

6) Reverse the corners inside.

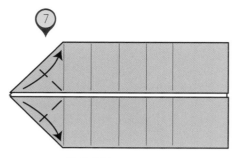

7) Fold two corners over.

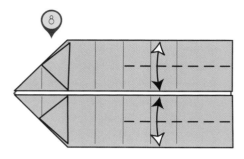

8) Crease and unfold twice.

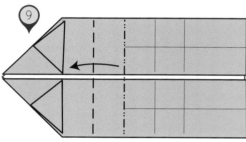

9) Make a pleat.

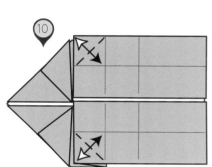

10) Fold and unfold two corners.

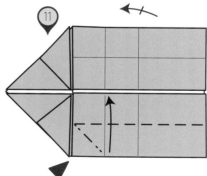

11) Fold the lower edge to the center, squashing the corner into a triangle. Repeat at the top.

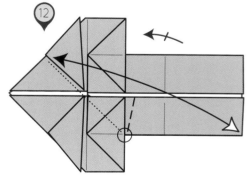

12) Fold starting at the circled corner so the lower left edge lies on the dotted line, then unfold. Repeat on the upper half. Turn the paper over.

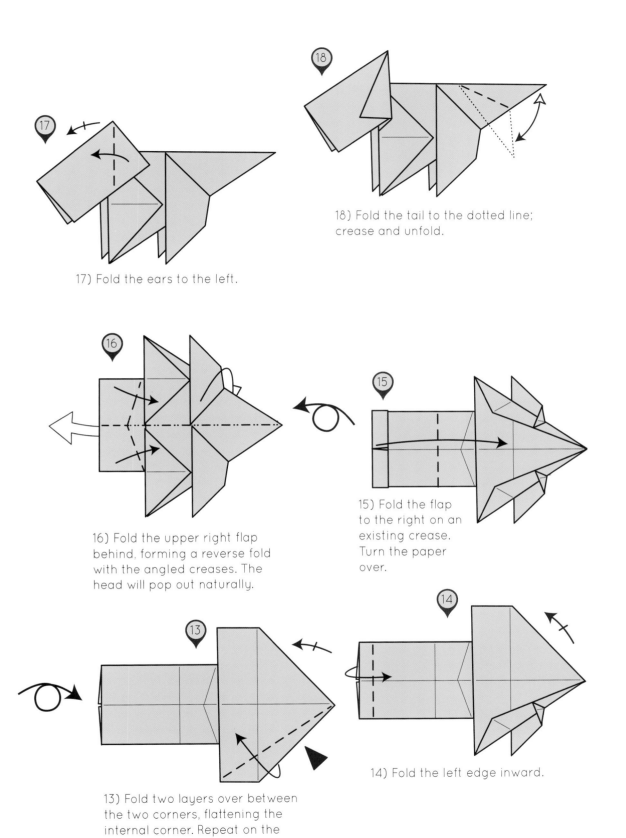

17) Fold the ears to the left.

18) Fold the tail to the dotted line; crease and unfold.

16) Fold the upper right flap behind, forming a reverse fold with the angled creases. The head will pop out naturally.

15) Fold the flap to the right on an existing crease. Turn the paper over.

13) Fold two layers over between the two corners, flattening the internal corner. Repeat on the upper half.

14) Fold the left edge inward.

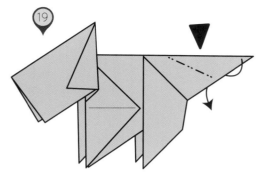

19) Reverse fold the tail inside.

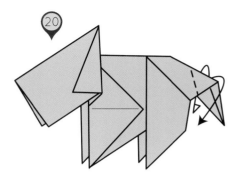

20) Wrap the tail flaps to the outside.

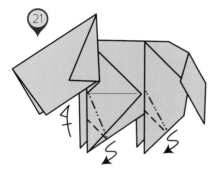

21) Shape the legs with firm mountain and valley creases.

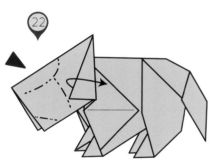

22) Open the ears half-way. Shape the head with gentle creases.

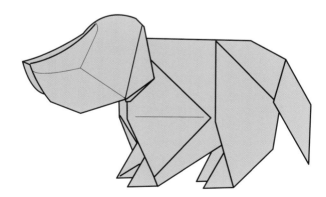

Patch the Dog

Román Díaz

An interesting sequence produces a dog full of character.
Focus on accurate creasing!

Size of the sheet: 7 x 7 in

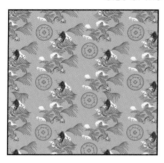

Paper

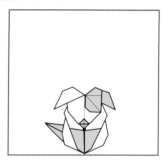

Relationship between
the paper and the origami

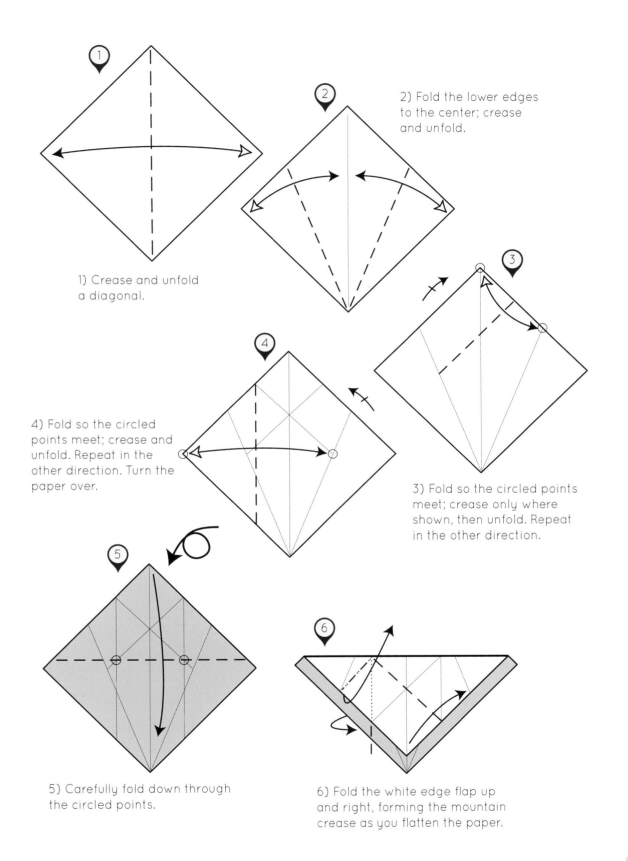

1) Crease and unfold a diagonal.

2) Fold the lower edges to the center; crease and unfold.

3) Fold so the circled points meet; crease only where shown, then unfold. Repeat in the other direction.

4) Fold so the circled points meet; crease and unfold. Repeat in the other direction. Turn the paper over.

5) Carefully fold down through the circled points.

6) Fold the white edge flap up and right, forming the mountain crease as you flatten the paper.

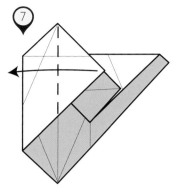

7) Fold a single corner to the left.

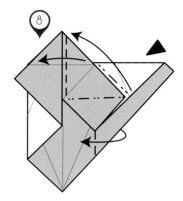

8) Make a similar move to step 6 in the other direction.

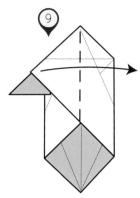

9) Fold a flap to the right.

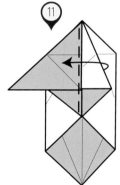

11) Fold a flap to the left.

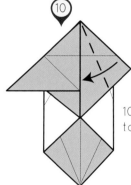

10) Fold the outer edge to the vertical center.

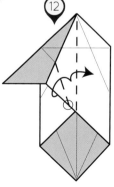

12) Make a valley to the circled point, then fold the flap over again.

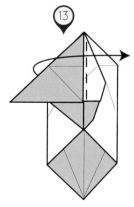

13) Fold the pink flap to the right.

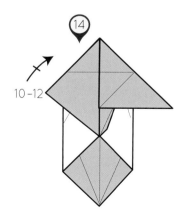

14) Repeat steps 10–12 on the left side.

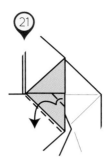

21) Fold over a small flap, then fold the rest of it over.

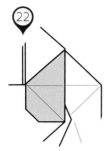

22) The result. Now we zoom out a little.

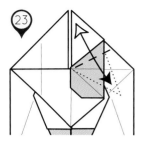

23) Fold the corner to the dotted line, then unfold.

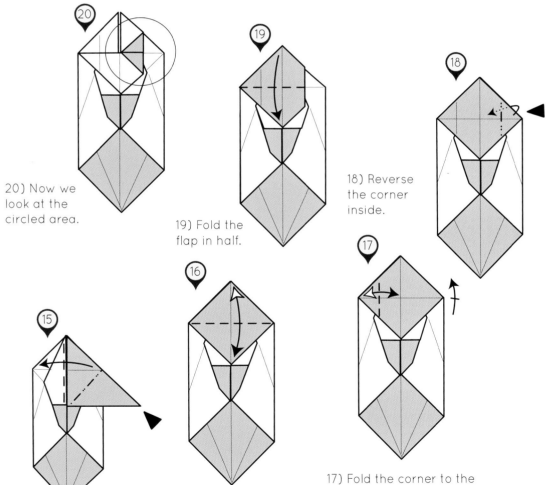

20) Now we look at the circled area.

19) Fold the flap in half.

18) Reverse the corner inside.

15) Lift and squash the pink flap.

16) Fold the colored square in half (upper layer only), then unfold.

17) Fold the corner to the center; crease and unfold. Repeat on the right.

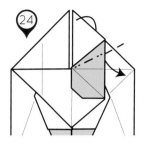

24) Reverse the corner inside.

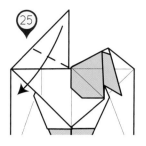

25) Fold the flap to match the other side.

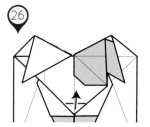

26) Fold up one corner to form the nose.

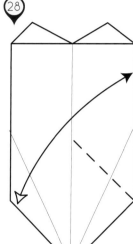
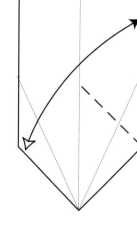

28) Crease only to the center, then unfold.

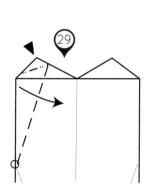

29) Fold the side in, carefully squashing flat at the top.

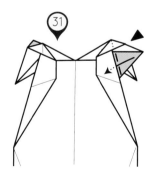

27) The result. Turn the paper over.

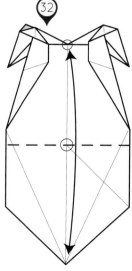

30) Repeat the last step on the right.

31) Fold the flap inside, reversing the top corner.

32) Fold through the circled point; crease and unfold.

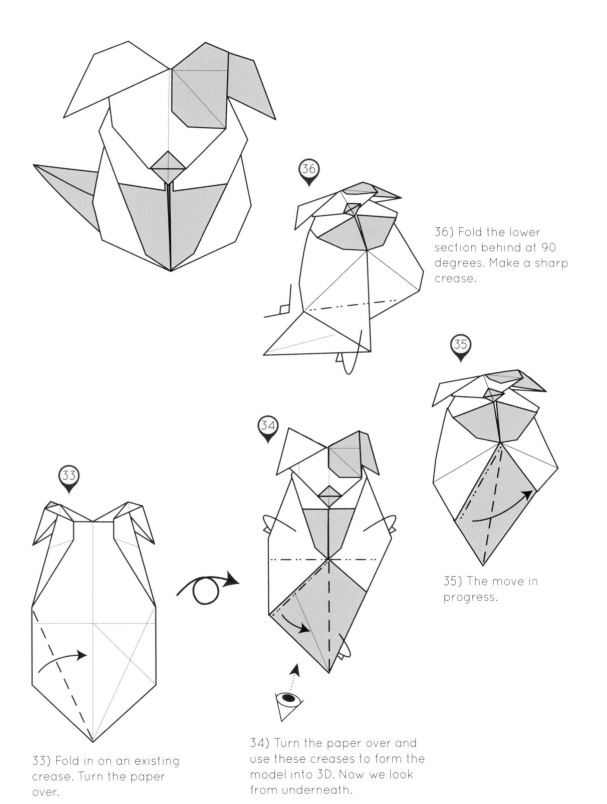

36) Fold the lower section behind at 90 degrees. Make a sharp crease.

35) The move in progress.

34) Turn the paper over and use these creases to form the model into 3D. Now we look from underneath.

33) Fold in on an existing crease. Turn the paper over.

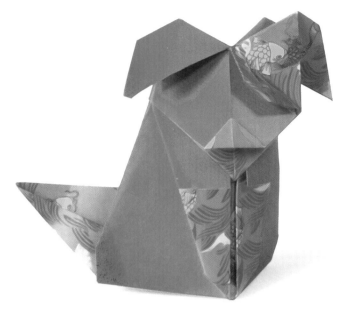

You Ain't Nothing but a Hound Dog

Nick Robinson

You will make a series of "pre-creases" before starting to actually fold the model. Try to be accurate.

Size of the sheet: 7 x 7 in

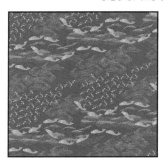

Paper

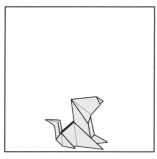

Relationship between
the paper and the origami

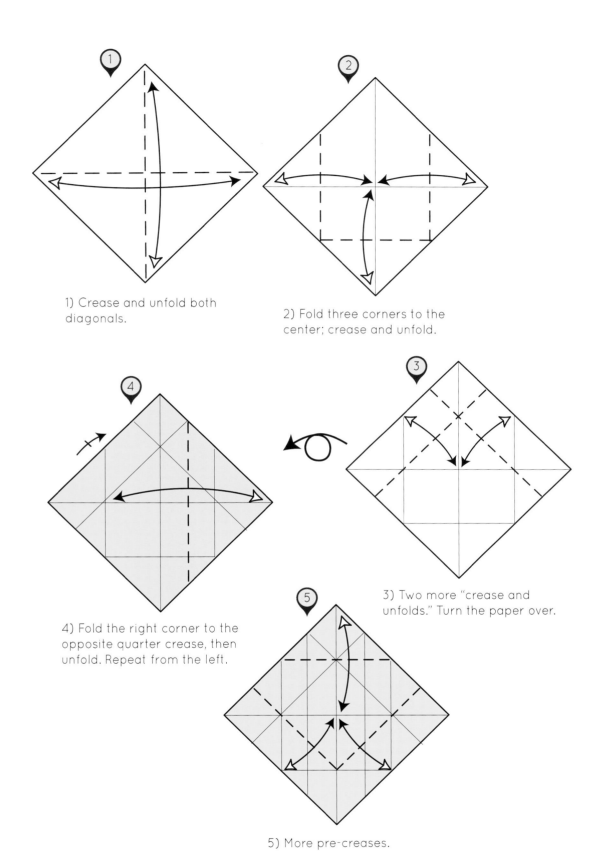

1) Crease and unfold both diagonals.

2) Fold three corners to the center; crease and unfold.

4) Fold the right corner to the opposite quarter crease, then unfold. Repeat from the left.

3) Two more "crease and unfolds." Turn the paper over.

5) More pre-creases.

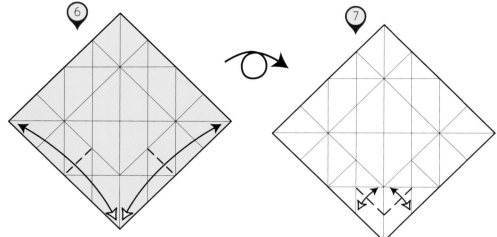

6) And more pre-creases!
Turn the paper over.

7) Guess what! The folding
starts soon.

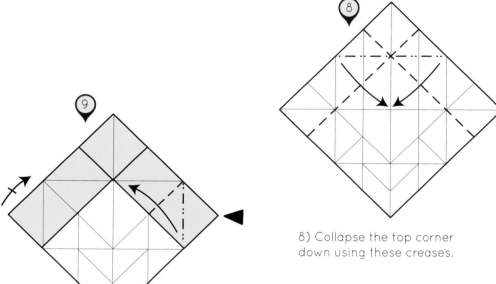

8) Collapse the top corner
down using these creases.

9) Fold the lower colored corner
over, flattening the right corner.
Repeat on the left side.

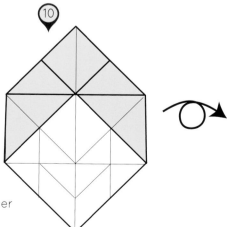

10) The result. Turn the paper
over from top to bottom.

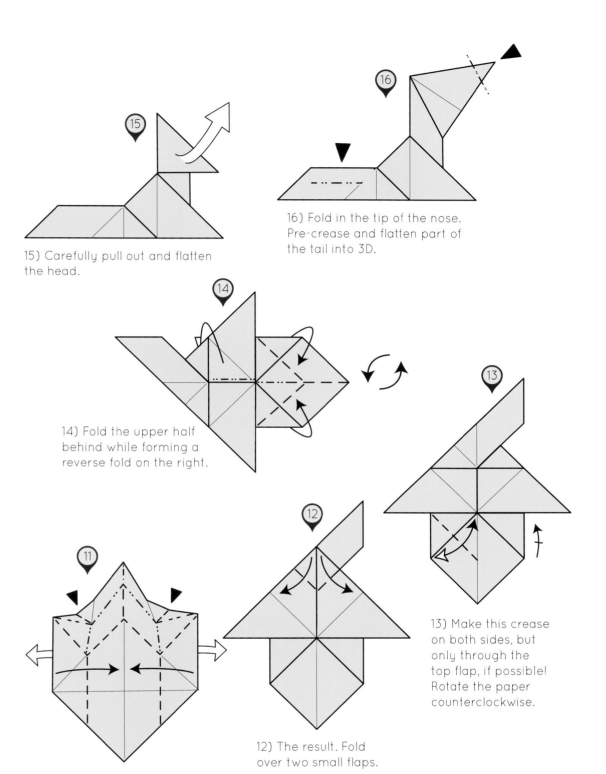

15) Carefully pull out and flatten the head.

16) Fold in the tip of the nose. Pre-crease and flatten part of the tail into 3D.

14) Fold the upper half behind while forming a reverse fold on the right.

13) Make this crease on both sides, but only through the top flap, if possible! Rotate the paper counterclockwise.

12) The result. Fold over two small flaps.

11) Begin to (slowly!) form these creases on the upper layer. Flaps flip out from underneath.

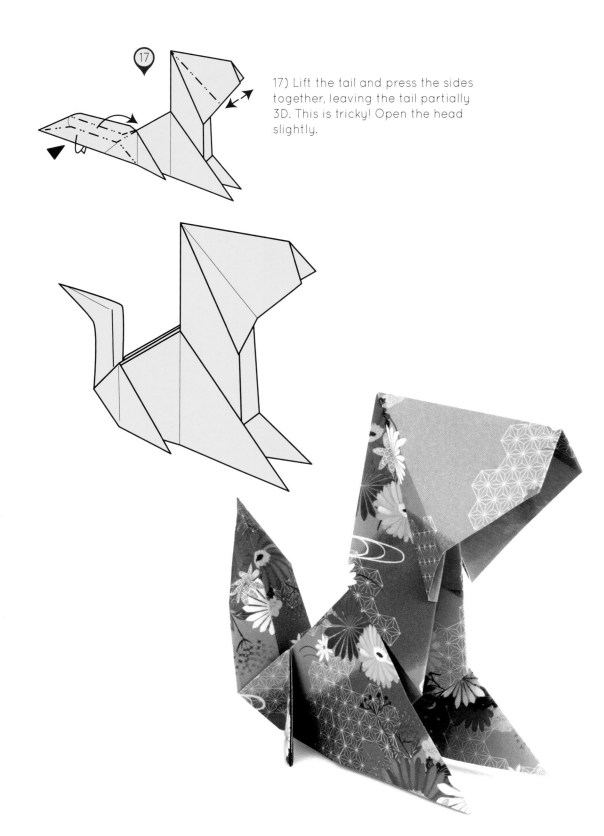

17) Lift the tail and press the sides together, leaving the tail partially 3D. This is tricky! Open the head slightly.

Perro Liberando

Luis Fernández Pérez

A sight we see too often on the streets, but when a dog has to go...
This model requires some care when folding—be prepared to make
several before you get it right.

Size of the sheet: 7 x 7 in

Paper

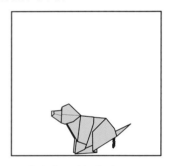

Relationship between
the paper and the origami

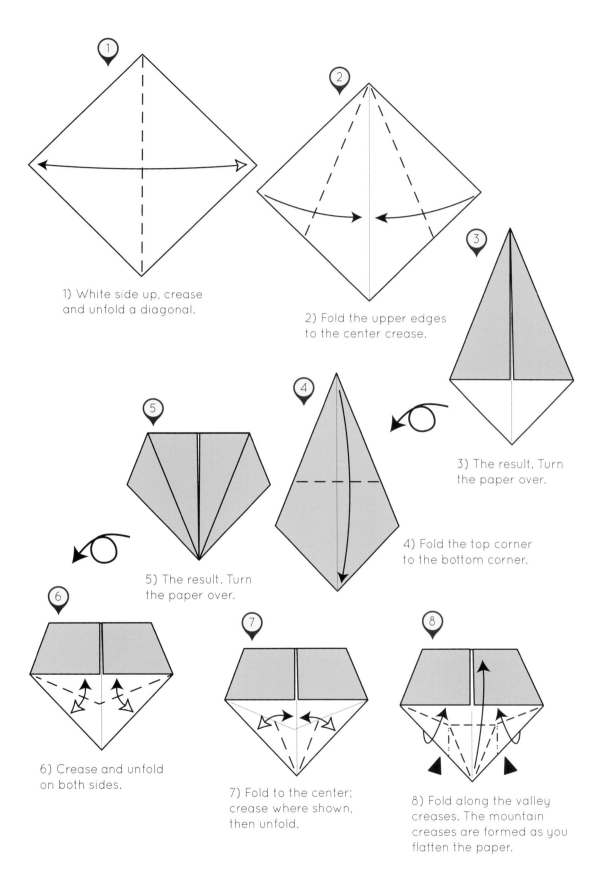

1) White side up, crease and unfold a diagonal.

2) Fold the upper edges to the center crease.

3) The result. Turn the paper over.

4) Fold the top corner to the bottom corner.

5) The result. Turn the paper over.

6) Crease and unfold on both sides.

7) Fold to the center; crease where shown, then unfold.

8) Fold along the valley creases. The mountain creases are formed as you flatten the paper.

123

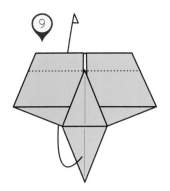

9) Fold the lower flap upward along the dotted line.

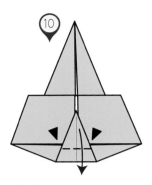

10) Fold the flap down, squashing the corners inside as you flatten the paper.

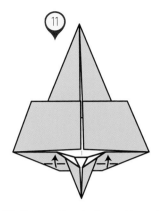

11) Swing the tail up, then fold the lower edge up as far as you can. Return the tail.

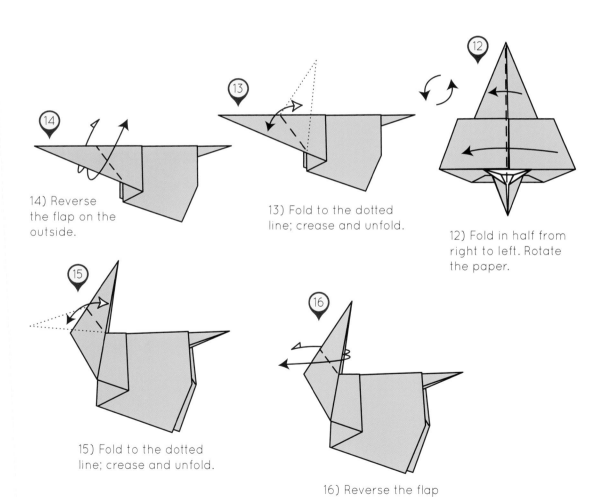

14) Reverse the flap on the outside.

13) Fold to the dotted line; crease and unfold.

12) Fold in half from right to left. Rotate the paper.

15) Fold to the dotted line; crease and unfold.

16) Reverse the flap to the outside.

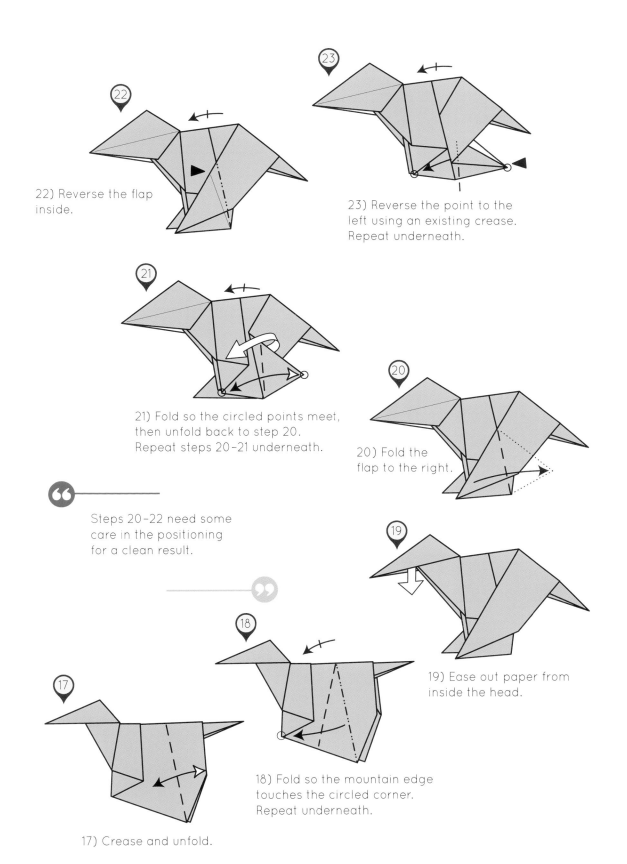

22) Reverse the flap inside.

23) Reverse the point to the left using an existing crease. Repeat underneath.

21) Fold so the circled points meet, then unfold back to step 20. Repeat steps 20–21 underneath.

Steps 20–22 need some care in the positioning for a clean result.

20) Fold the flap to the right.

19) Ease out paper from inside the head.

18) Fold so the mountain edge touches the circled corner. Repeat underneath.

17) Crease and unfold.

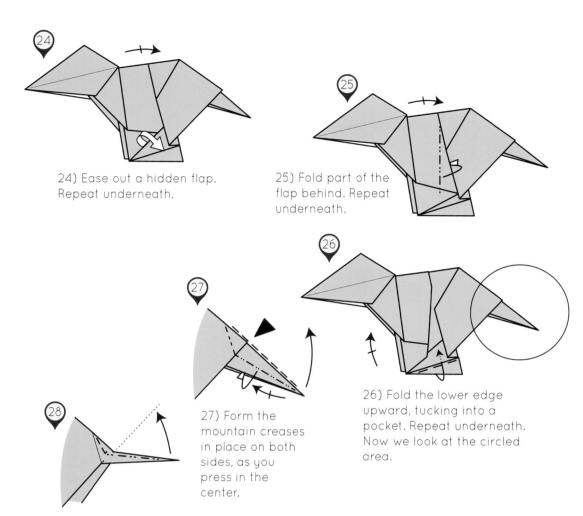

24) Ease out a hidden flap. Repeat underneath.

25) Fold part of the flap behind. Repeat underneath.

26) Fold the lower edge upward, tucking into a pocket. Repeat underneath. Now we look at the circled area.

27) Form the mountain creases in place on both sides, as you press in the center.

28) The tail narrows and rises to the dotted line. Press flat to fix in place.

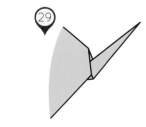

29) The tail is complete.

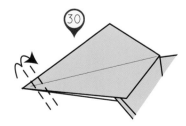

30) Open the nose and wrap a small point over twice.

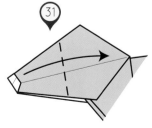

31) Fold the flap to the right. Don't crease firmly.

126

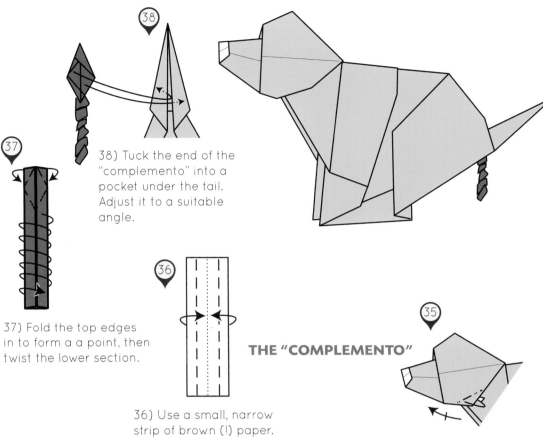

38) Tuck the end of the "complemento" into a pocket under the tail. Adjust it to a suitable angle.

37) Fold the top edges in to form a a point, then twist the lower section.

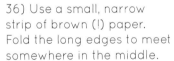

THE "COMPLEMENTO"

36) Use a small, narrow strip of brown (!) paper. Fold the long edges to meet somewhere in the middle.

35) Shape the head to taste on both sides.

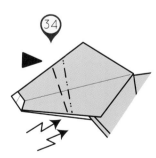

34) Reverse the nose inside on the creases you have made.

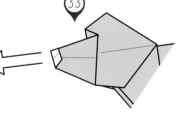

33) When you are happy with the shape of the face, flatten the creases, then unfold.

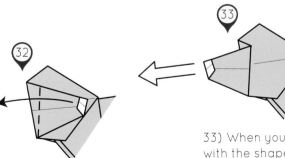

32) Fold the flap back at an angle. Again, don't flatten.

Bulldog

Jacky Chan

This is the most difficult design in the book, so be prepared
to make it several times before you get a neat result.
Start with a larger sheet of paper.

Size of the sheet: 7 x 7 in

Paper

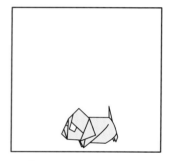

Relationship between
the paper and the origami

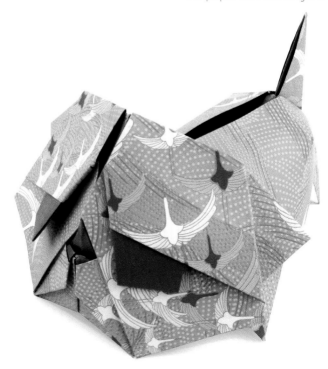

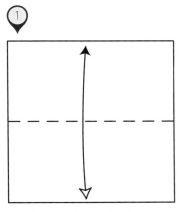

1) White side up; fold in half, crease and unfold.

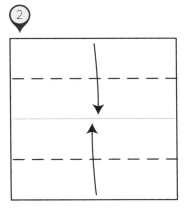

2) Fold upper and lower edges to the center.

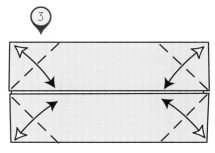

3) Fold all four corners in; crease and unfold.

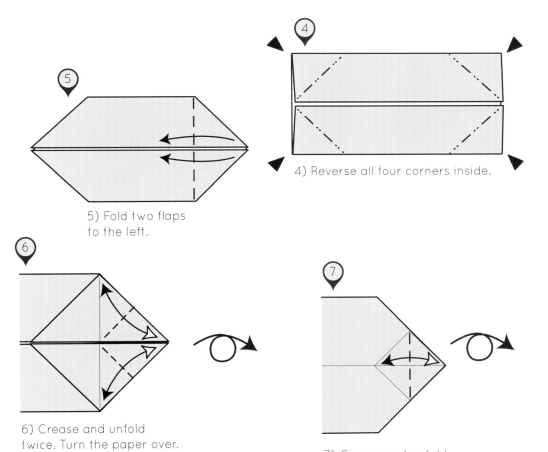

4) Reverse all four corners inside.

5) Fold two flaps to the left.

6) Crease and unfold twice. Turn the paper over.

7) Crease and unfold. Turn the paper over.

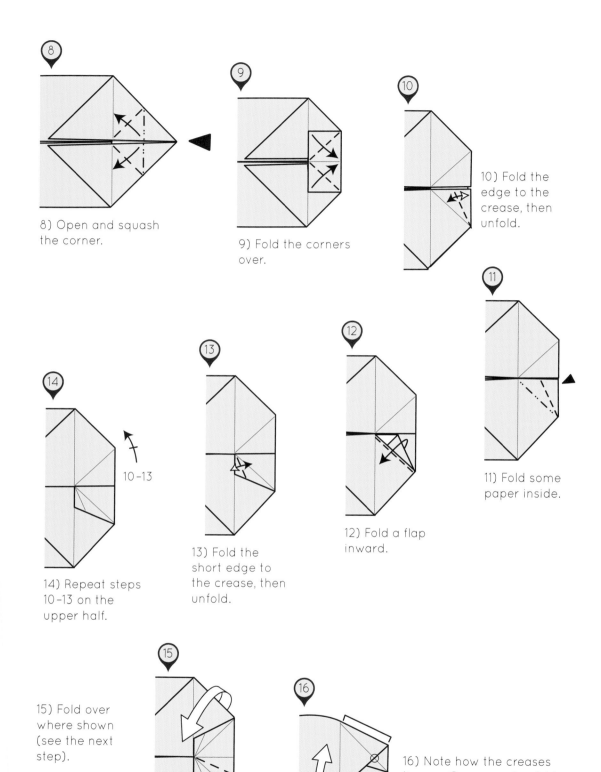

8) Open and squash the corner.

9) Fold the corners over.

10) Fold the edge to the crease, then unfold.

11) Fold some paper inside.

12) Fold a flap inward.

13) Fold the short edge to the crease, then unfold.

14) Repeat steps 10–13 on the upper half.

10–13

15) Fold over where shown (see the next step).

16) Note how the creases line up. Crease and unfold.

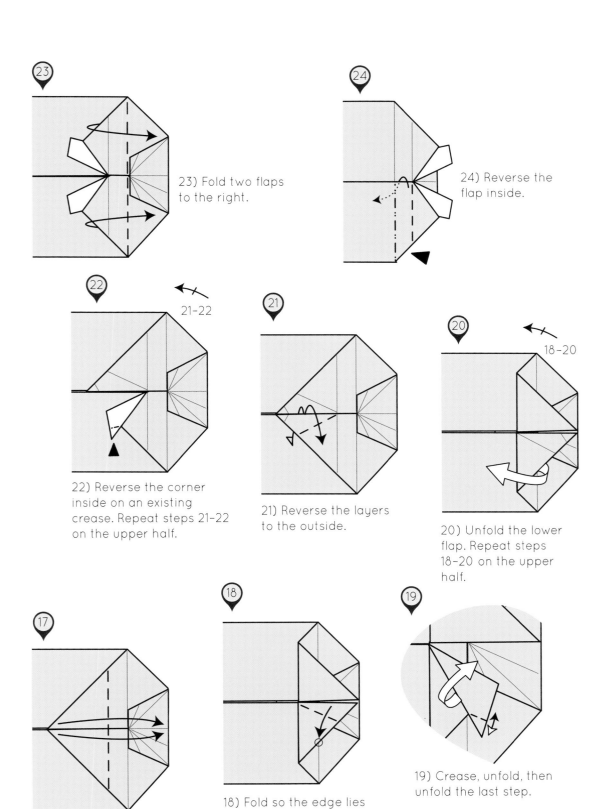

23) Fold two flaps to the right.

24) Reverse the flap inside.

22) Reverse the corner inside on an existing crease. Repeat steps 21–22 on the upper half.

21) Reverse the layers to the outside.

20) Unfold the lower flap. Repeat steps 18–20 on the upper half.

17) Fold the inner corners to the right edge.

18) Fold so the edge lies on the circled point.

19) Crease, unfold, then unfold the last step.

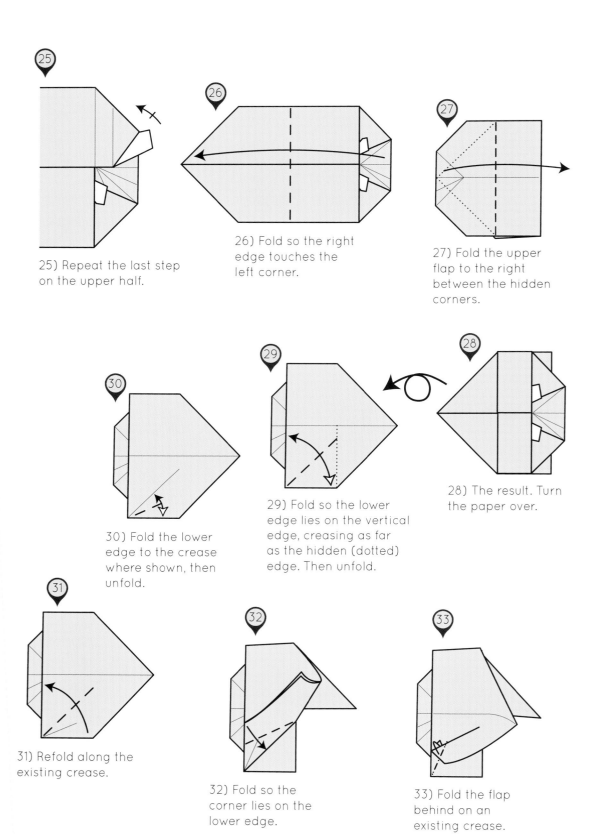

25) Repeat the last step on the upper half.

26) Fold so the right edge touches the left corner.

27) Fold the upper flap to the right between the hidden corners.

28) The result. Turn the paper over.

29) Fold so the lower edge lies on the vertical edge, creasing as far as the hidden (dotted) edge. Then unfold.

30) Fold the lower edge to the crease where shown, then unfold.

31) Refold along the existing crease.

32) Fold so the corner lies on the lower edge.

33) Fold the flap behind on an existing crease.

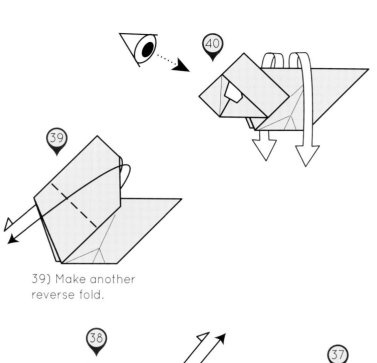

40) Open the paper, but leave the creases in place as much as you can. The eye shows the next viewpoint.

39) Make another reverse fold.

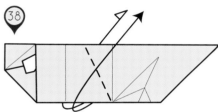

38) Reverse the left side of the paper to the right.

37) Fold the lower edge to the crease, then unfold.

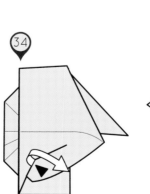

34) Press these folds firmly, then unfold so the paper is flat.

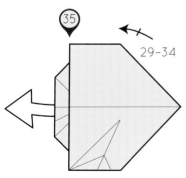

29–34

35) Repeat steps 29–34 on the upper half, then pull out the lower flap.

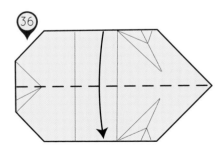

36) Fold in half downward.

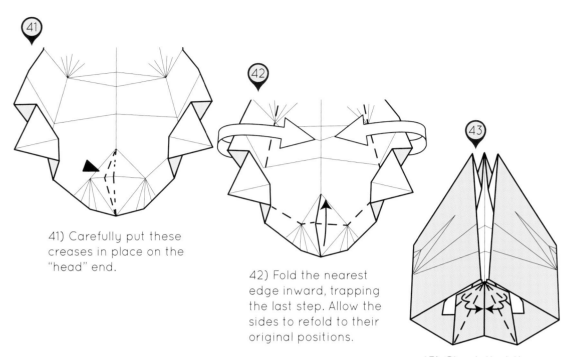

41) Carefully put these creases in place on the "head" end.

42) Fold the nearest edge inward, trapping the last step. Allow the sides to refold to their original positions.

43) Check that the folds made in steps 11–12 are in the right place. Fold the upper edges over and over.

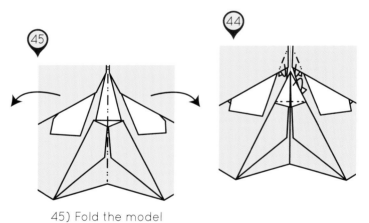

45) Fold the model in half again.

44) Fold the white tip of the nose behind. Fold in two small corners above the eyes and crease them firmly.

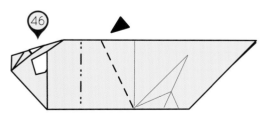

46) Reform the two reverse folds (originally made in steps 38–39).

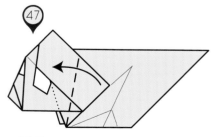

47) Fold the lower edge of the ear to lie on the hidden (dotted) edge.

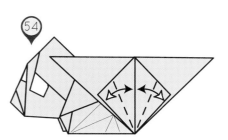

54) Fold the lower edges of the square section to the vertical center; crease firmly and unfold.

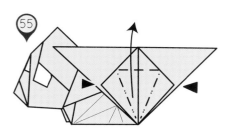

55) Fold the lower corner upward, folding the side corners inward.

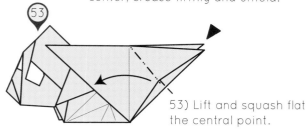

53) Lift and squash flat the central point.

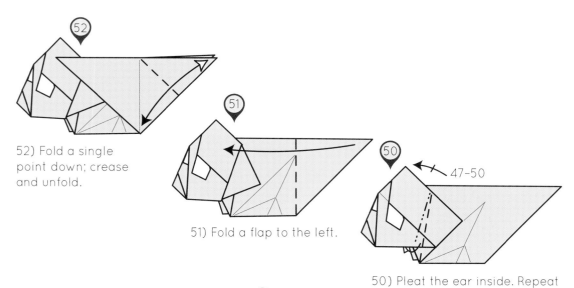

52) Fold a single point down; crease and unfold.

51) Fold a flap to the left.

47-50

50) Pleat the ear inside. Repeat steps 47-50 on the other ear.

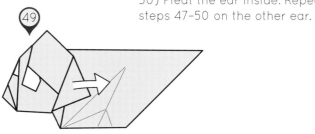

49) Unfold the ear flap.

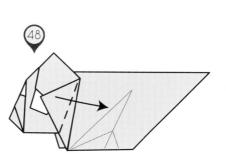

48) Fold the ear flap to the right.

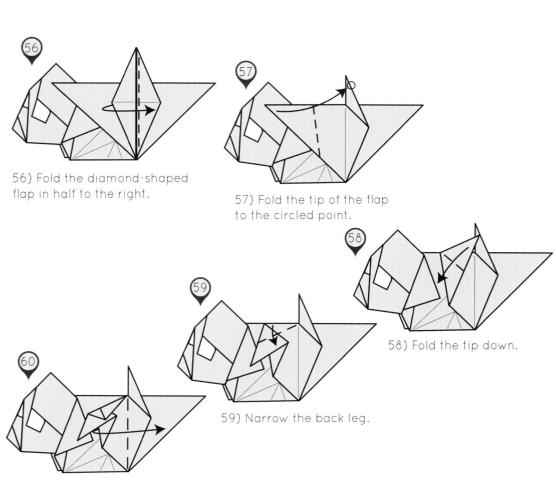

56) Fold the diamond-shaped flap in half to the right.

57) Fold the tip of the flap to the circled point.

58) Fold the tip down.

59) Narrow the back leg.

60) Swing the flap to the right.

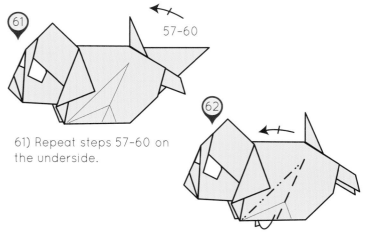

57–60

61) Repeat steps 57–60 on the underside.

62) Reform steps 31–33 on both sides, making the body 3D. The legs wrap around slightly.

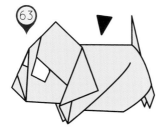

63) Press the back slightly to help round the body.

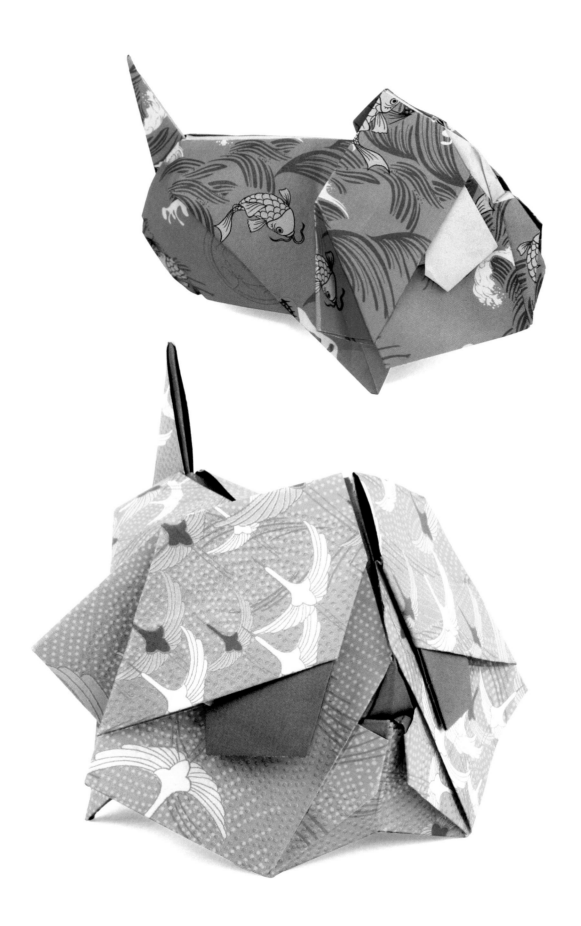

Biographies

NICK ROBINSON - Dog in a Kennel - Bone - Nodding Dog - Alison's Dog - Minimal Dog -
You Ain't Nothing but a Hound Dog

He is a professional paper artist and has written over 70 books on the subject. He was awarded the *Sidney French medal* by the British Origami Society for his outstanding contribution to origami. He is also an honorary member of the Society. He has taught and lectured on origami all around the world, including America, Ireland, France, Hungary, Germany, Austria, Switzerland, Spain, Italy, the United Arab Emirates and Japan. Nick is the author of the following books published by Dover Publications: *Origami Anywhere*, *Butterflies in Origami*, and *Cats in Origami*.

AKIRA YOSHIZAWA - Yoshizawa's Dog

A Japanese origami artist, he is considered to be the grandmaster of origami. He is credited with raising origami from a craft to a living art. Yoshizawa acted as an international cultural ambassador for Japan throughout his career. In 1983, Emperor Hirohito awarded him the Order of the Rising Sun, one of the highest honors bestowed in Japan.

ROBERT NEALE - Scotty Dog

He has been designing origami since the '60s, is recognized worldwide as a creator of superb designs, and has worked in the field of modular origami. He is a prominent member of OrigamiUSA. He was one of the first academicians in the U.S. to study the hospice movement and was ordained by the United Church of Christ. Robert grew up in Detroit, Michigan.

GAY MERRILL GROSS - Woof! Woof! Puppy - Gay's Dog

She is an expert in origami and the related skill of napkin folding. She works with simple designs and is the author of *Origami: The Art of Paperfolding*, *The Art of Napkin Folding*, *Folding Napkins*, *Napkin Folds for Special Occasions* and three introductory books on origami. Gay lives in New York City.

EDWIN CORRIE - Alsatian

A British creator, currently living in France, Edwin has a unique "geometric" style that makes his designs easily recognizable. He creates using both squares and rectangles and his work is admired worldwide. He has had several collections of his work published by the British Origami Society as well as in commercial books.

MARC KIRSCHENBAUM - Kirschenbaum's Dog

He is an American origami artist, designer, and board member of OrigamiUSA. He is known for creation of complex origami models, including various instrumentalists, insects, and erotic origami works. Marc's published books include *Paper in Harmony*, *Origami Bugs*, and *Erotic Origami*.

SHOKO AOYAGI - Dog - Puppy

She was born in Japan and is a very inspiring and creative teacher. She brings an original perspective to origami art and her work is often simple yet effective. She has led origami workshops in Sydney at primary schools and kindergartens. In 2004, Shoko led the Origami workshop at the Sydney Opera House to celebrate Asian arts.

TONY O'HARE - Dawg

A British creator based in Bristol, Tony has been a creator of designs for 30 years, mainly animals and birds. He is famous for creating the very first "origami nude." He has had several collections of his work published by the British Origami Society. Tony is currently the Chairman of the Society and has been awarded their *Sidney French Medal*.

BODO HAAG - Bodo's Dog

Bodo comes from Tübingen, Germany. He discovered origami at 5 years old. At 8, he designed his first model, a crow. In the same year, he attended a small origami meeting near Munich. Since then, he has continued to design models and attend conventions. He prefers to fold animals and is currently working on super-complex models.

ROMÁN DÍAZ - Patch the Dog

Born in Montevideo, Uruguay, he has lived in Argentina, Honduras, and Mozambique. Fascinated by the possibilities of origami, he started designing his own models. By 2005 his animal designs were attracting international attention. Since then Román has been a special guest at origami conventions in Spain, France, Italy, Germany, and Chile and has published two books.

LUIS FERNÁNDEZ PÉREZ - Perro Liberando

Luis is one of the most prolific Spanish origami artist. His two great hobbies are mathematics and origami. He is an honorary member of Centro Latino de Origami (Peru). He is highly skilled in both creating new designs and folding them beautifully.

JACKY CHAN - Bulldog

Jacky lives in Hong Kong and has an international following. His designs are always unusual and ingenious and have a unique character that you can easily recognize, a rare talent in the world of origami.